HEADLINE PHOTOGRAPHY

HEADLINE PHOTOGRAPHY

The pictures that made the news

HAROLD EVANS

TREASURE PRESS

*A list of the photographers whose work
appears in this book, and the roll of World Press Photo
jury members, will be found on pages 206–7*

The 1980 jury for the World Press Photo awards promenades among the thousands of prints from which they will choose the winners

First published in the Great Britain in 1981 by
Quiller Press Ltd under the title *Eyewitness 2*

This revised edition published in 1985

Published in 1990 by
Treasure Press
Michelin House
81 Fulham Road
London SW3 6RB

ISBN 1 85051 581 6

Printed in Portugal

First edition designed by Michael Rand and John Tennant
Captions and assistance to Harold Evans by Neil Hepburn

Final 16 pages of this edition written by Hugo Frost and designed by Jim Reader

A CELEBRATION OF WORLD PRESS PHOTO

photo: Ruud Taal

**The International Jury 1985 of World Press Photo.
Seated from left to right: Christian Caujolle (Libération – France), Patricia Seppällä, president (Lehtikuva Oy – Finland), Howard Chapnick (Black Star – U.S.A.).
Standing from left to right: Colin Jacobson (Observer** Magazine – U.K.), Istvàn Bara (M.T.I. – Hungary), Friso Endt (NRC – The Netherlands), Yuri Golovjatenko (Novosty – U.S.S.R.), Vincent Mentzel, secretary, Per Mortensen (Mortensen's Forlag – Norway), Heinz Morstadt (Bunte Illustrierte – F.R.G.).

This magnificent book celebrates the 30th anniversary of the World Press Photo Holland Foundation. The Amsterdam-based non-profit-making organisation was founded in 1956 when three Amsterdam photographers, Ben van Meerendonk sr., Kees Scherer and Bram Wisman, expanded Holland's national competition for the Press Photo of the Year into an international one. It remains an idealistic organisation, created by press photographers for press photographers, fully independent and unaffected by the political blocks of a divided world.

The activities of World Press Photo are initiated and directed by the Stichting (Foundation) World Press Photo Holland under the high patronage of His Royal Highness Prince Bernhard of the Netherlands.

It is the aim of the Foundation to invoke and promote world-wide interest in press photography as an important means of furthering international understanding. It tries to achieve this by organising the annual contest, the exhibitions, symposia and conferences relating to press photography.

The Foundation is an independent, cultural and non-profit-making organisation, which enjoys the support of the Netherlands Government, the City of Amsterdam and a group of Friends of World Press Photo.

World Press Photo's Golden Eye prizes are often called the 'Oscars' of press photography.

The contest is the only world-wide meeting place for press photography and gains its importance mainly from the importance and integrity of its independent international jury.

For that reason we dedicate this book to members past and present of the World Press Photo juries.

Joop Swart, President
World Press Photo Holland Foundation

THE PICTURES THAT MADE THE NEWS

When the era represented by this book opens immense dramas agitate the air. Three wars are to come to the Middle East. More coups than you can count are being hatched in Africa and Latin America. Thriving Lebanon is doomed to dismemberment; Cyprus, Northern Ireland, Nigeria and Pakistan are fused for civil war. Peace may be coming to Vietnam but so is genocide in Cambodia. Seven American Presidents will stand on Capitol Hill and take the oath of office, one of them not long afterwards to lie nearby in a military grave, the victim of an assassin's bullet. Another will depart in ignominy, the first President to resign, with a wave from the helicopter on the White House lawn. There is magic too. At the beginning man is bound to his planet. At the end he has walked in space, motored on the moon, and taken pictures of Mars, Jupiter, Venus and Saturn. Nuclear fission which had produced only the bomb is boiling the breakfast egg, the laser is discovered, the human heart transplanted, a baby is conceived in a test tube; businessmen go to New York for lunch at twice the speed of sound and come back to Europe for dinner, and every schoolgirl's satchel carries a digital calculator.

In 1956 we are saying farewell to Churchill. Stalin is dead, succeeded by Bulganin and Khruschev and the trumpets are about to sound for Charles de Gaulle, President of the Fifth Republic of France. An astonishing cast of characters waits to march onto the proscenium of history. Castro will soon emerge from the mountains to seize power in Cuba, George Papadopoulos and his comic opera colonels rehearse in Greece, and ambition we will regret stirs in Idi Amin and Bokassa. There is the flying doctor of diplomacy, Henry Kissinger, and the mesmeric Archbishop Makarios, and the irrepressible Mrs Gandhi. The fifteenth Islamic century dawns and with it the Ayatollah Khomeini. Many, as well as the Shah, are marked men: King Faisal of Iraq, Presidents Somoza of Nicaragua, Karume of Zanzibar, Mujibur Rahman of Bangladesh and Allende of Chile, are all murdered. It is an era of political terrorism, claiming the black martyrs Steve Biko and Martin Luther King as well as Italy's Moro and Britain's Mountbatten. There are predictable events which please – Queen Elizabeth of England, four years on the throne in 1956, celebrates her triumphant silver jubilee – and others which astound and enchant. Pope Paul VI amazes the world by embarking on a series of unprecedented pilgrimages for peace: the first taking him to the land of Christ's birth and death where no Pope since Peter had ever set foot. And nobody in 1956 could have foreseen Sadat and Begin embracing in Jerusalem or China-baiter Richard Nixon taking tea with Mao Tse-Tung.

This book collapses time. Its images of these 25 years of our history do not merely remind us of events. They each of them instantly carry us back into the very atmosphere of the moment, reawakening its emotions and its reflections. Who can look again at the photograph of Lee Harvey Oswald, the killer of President John Kennedy, dying himself at gunpoint, without feeling the ache of those dead days of the Sixties or deny the naïve excitement when at the end of the decade an American called Neil Armstrong set foot on the moon and, like any other tourist, posed for a snapshot? So powerful is the appeal to memory that many of us will be able to remember even the occasion when we saw these images for the first time. And anyone who did not live through those days and perhaps sees the pictures for the first time in the pages of this book will never be able entirely to forget them. Another 25 years from now – I promise, money back if not satisfied – it will require only a moment to recall on the retina of the mind Don McCullin's photograph of the orphan boy in Cyprus piteously stretching his hand to his newly widowed mother, or Hyunh Con Ut's of the children burned by napalm running down the road in Vietnam, or Françoise Demulder's of a woman pleading with a gunman in Beirut.

It is very curious. Each photograph is only a small, flat

1963. The death of Oswald: the picture as key to total recall

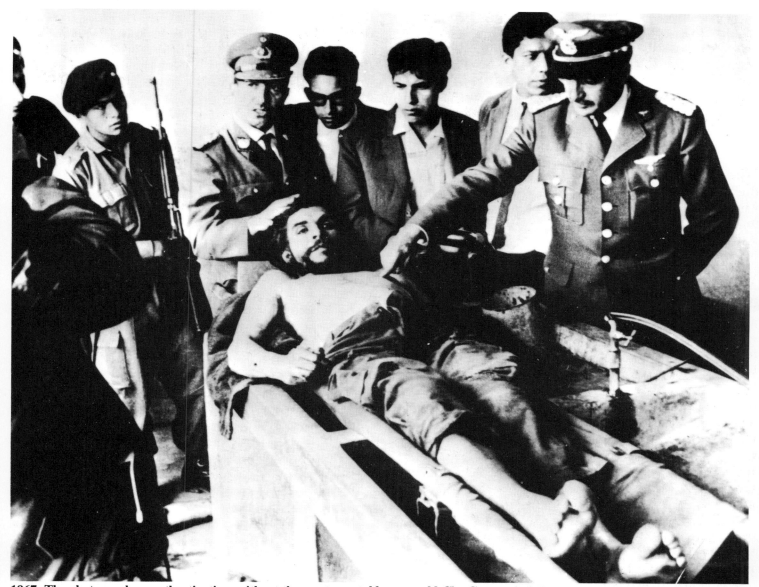

1967. The photograph as authentication: without the mortuary tableau, would Che Guevara's followers have believed he was dead?

series of tones from black to white. Its depth is an illusion, its animation symbolic. Yet it has this mysterious richness transcending all its limitations so that our impressions of major and complex events may be permanently fashioned by a single news photograph. The photograph's power lies in the unique quality epitomised by Marvin Krone – that it preserves forever a finite fraction of the infinite time of the universe. It is no accident that one of the most effective techniques in the supposedly competitive media of television and the cinema is to freeze a frame of the moving sequence. Life itself seems to be suspended; and we find it easier to absorb and recall this isolated moment than a succession of images.

That was why John le Carré reviewing the work of McCullin found himself saying he would rather watch any amount of television footage than be forced to leaf through McCullin's albums of human suffering; and why *The New York Times* did not in 1965 publish the photograph by

Malcolm Browne of a monk setting himself alight in a street in Saigon to protest at the alleged persecution of Buddhists by the Vietnamese government. Photojournalism does raise anxieties; and they particularly have to be acknowledged in a book celebrating 25 years of achievement, with some photographs of surpassing horror including that one. There are several areas of debate: the effects of portraying violence, the capacity of a single image to substitute emotion for analysis and the claims of conscience on a photographer.

The editor of *The New York Times* simply did not think the picture of the burning monk was fit for the breakfast tables of Americans. When the American Society of Newspaper Editors asked editors round the country what they thought of that decision, the editor of the Syracuse paper said an editor who would not use that picture would not have a run on the Cruxifixion. Today it does seem a curious decision, yet it has to be recognised that pictures like this do distress and do require justification, and that there is a danger that a daily diet of ever more extreme brutality will atrophy our sense of outrage. It is no secret that this is something which has often concerned World Press Photo jurors from the Soviet Union and Eastern Europe. The most cursory examination of the yearbooks will confirm that this book's selection is not unbalanced – violence is the leitmotif of the era – but for any single photograph three tests suggest themselves: Is the event portrayed of such social or historic significance that the shock of the viewer is justified? Is the violent detail necessary for a proper understanding of the event? Is it necessary for corroboration? These tests exclude much gratuitous offence. There is no justification for reproducing the severed head of film star Jayne Mansfield killed in a road crash and no editor did so. There is no justification for photographing the corpse of Lee Harvey Oswald, crudely stitched up again on the pathologist's post-mortem table, and only the *National Enquirer* did that. But equally it is right to take and print the photograph reproduced in this volume of the Kurdish rebels being shot down by a firing squad in Iran and that of the police chief executing a prisoner in a Saigon street: the most important gunshot of the Vietnam war not because it was heard round the world but because it was *seen*.

The shock from the content of that photograph is so considerable that it prompts in parallel a whole new set of questions. Photojournalism, much more than written jour-

1965. Burning monk: should the photographer have stopped it?

nalism, is bound to be random; it requires a man with a camera to be on the scene at the time and to be able to record the news moment. That is part of the excitement of photojournalism, the sense of being there; it is also a liability. Most of the photographs which decorated the pages of the world's newspapers from the Spanish Civil War were faked; as much as 90 per cent of the Abyssinian photo-coverage, Herbert Matthews has estimated, was staged by photographers kept away from the front.

Vietnam was the most authentically photographed (and thereby perhaps the most controversial) war of all time; but it was all from one side. While the Americans exposed themselves to the camera, few correspondents, let alone photographers, were allowed to visit areas controlled by North Vietnam. When *The New York Times* published the Adams picture it sought to maintain its renowned balance by accompanying it with a photograph of an atrocity on a child by the Vietcong. It was an awkward solution but it was correct in recognising the power of the photograph and the responsibility arriving with it. There is no escaping the dilemmas this may bring, it seems to me by the patronising attitude of John Szarkowski of New York's Museum of Modern Art. "Photography's failure to explain large public issues has become increasingly clear," he writes. "No photographs from the Vietnam war – neither Donald McCullin's stomach-wrenching documents of atrocity and horror nor the late Larry Burrows's superb and disturbingly conventional battle scenes – begin to serve either as explication or symbol for that enormity." Explanation, no, but as a symbol surely it was the photographs which burned themselves into our minds? And to discuss photojournalism in these dismissive terms is to neglect its compelling authority in description, documentation and corroboration. We believe what we see; and only what we believe can become a public issue. Jacob Riis discovered and demonstrated that for all time in New York in 1888 when he wrote about the sweatshops and slums and nobody believed they were as bad as he said. He had to teach himself to use a camera and invent documentary photography to prove his point. It is one of the central contributions of photojournalism that it goes beyond the limits of imagination. It makes the unbelievable believable. George Rodger, William Vandivert, Johnny Florea and Margaret Bourke-White and others showed us in 1945, by indelible photographs, what it meant to be a Jew in Auschwitz and Dachau. Until then the reports about Hitler's death camps were only half believed and even today, such was the enormity of the crimes, we need photographs to convince us that, yes, it really did happen.

It was the photographs of U.S. army man Ronald Haeberle, taken on 16th May 1968, and only published 18 months later, which carried the conviction that a massacre had indeed taken place at the village of My Lai. More recently only the photographs of the victims brought home

1972. The photograph unforgettably encapsulates our history

the stunning realisation that 900 people really had poisoned themselves in a mass suicide in Guyana. Likewise when the world thought that Mao was dead he proved he was alive by being photographed swimming in the Yangtse river and Che Guevara was only indisputably dead when we were invited to look at that famous elegiac photograph with an officer pointing to the fatal bullet hole. Conversely, we can gauge the value of photojournalism by its absence. The reality of the trench warfare in World War I, which we sense so well today, was obscured from the populations at the time because the photographs were never published. And what happened in our period to the people of Cambodia at the hands of the Khmer Rouge is imperfectly comprehended round the world because words literally fail us; the few photographs we have now are merely the half-remembered images of a nightmare.

Despite the difficulties and the erratic nature of the photographic vision, therefore, it is impossible to go along with Szarkowski when he concludes "most issues of importance cannot be photographed". On the contrary, some issues of importance can only be understood through photography. How better, one wonders, can we at a distance understand the reality of mercury poisoning at Minamata than by Eugene Smith's pictures of the pollution, and the crippled children?

This book then, as well as linking us to our past, is a very necessary tribute to our photojournalists. People are inclined to think of the photographer, as Wilson Hicks wrote, as a gross, near-simian fellow with a press card in the band of his battered hat and a big cigar in his mouth.

Turning the pages of a photographic collection we do not, many of us, have an instinctive sense of the risks, the hardships, the struggles with conscience which lie behind the image. When we look at the photograph in this book of the priest giving absolution to a dying marine in Venezuela in 1962 we are distanced, invulnerable and

unknowing. Hector Rondon Lavero, who took the photograph, was differently placed: "I found myself in solid lead for forty-five minutes. I was flattened against the wall while the bullets were flying when the priest appeared. The truth is I don't know how I took those pictures. Lying on the ground I just began shooting pictures while the bullets were whistling." Many have risked their lives, and too many have lost them, in pursuit to capture an image they believe will reveal a universal truth and hold it fast forever. "If your pictures aren't good enough you are not close enough," in the words of the great Robert Capa, who died on a landmine in Vietnam.

In the Lebanon several photographers, like Catherine LeRoy, were threatened by gunmen: "You shoot, I shoot." In Cambodia Philip Jones Griffiths spent two terrifying hours in a foxhole bombarded by the Khmer Rouge, only to have the best roll of film ruined in the darkroom.

There are many agonising self-appraisals. Two photographers walked away rather than record the bayonetting of Biharis on the Dacca polo field. Clive Limpkin has described his mental torture when, as a photographer in Ulster determined to be completely impartial, he hesitated to shout when some IRA men tried to gun down three British soldiers standing in the distance.

Peter Arnett, who photographed a Buddhist monk ablaze, beat off the Vietnamese secret police trying to take his camera and sent his photograph round the world, later reflected: "I could have prevented the immolation by rushing at him and kicking the gasoline away. As a human being I wanted to, as a reporter I couldn't." Professional detachment comes hard. When five pressmen were machine gunned by the Vietcong in May 1968, Charlie Eggleston, the UPI photographer, could stand it no longer. He went out one day with a weapon and never came back.

But perhaps the last word, before we turn to the volume's legacy of 25 years of endeavours, should be with Philip Jones Griffiths, one of the most compassionate of the Vietnam war photographers. "You cannot focus," he has said, "with tears in your eyes. We cannot help feeling involved. But we have to steel ourselves. Our job is to record it all for history."

1976. Would we understand their pain without their pictures?

1956: IMPERIAL PUNISHMENTS

EXTRA

Mirror News

BRITISH BOMB
5 EGYPT CITIES

Incendiaries Dropped in Combined Sea-Air Action

This is the watershed year. The photograph marks the slow unravelling of the Second World War. But new convulsions are imminent. In June Colonel Abdul Nasser is elected President of Egypt and six weeks later the United States Secretary of State, John Foster Dulles, angered by Nasser's burgeoning links with the Soviet Union, withdraws money from the projected high dam at Aswan. Britain follows suit. On July 27, anniversary of Egypt's revolution, Nasser retaliates. He nationalises the Suez Canal which the British and French regard as their jugular vein. It is the countdown to war. Sir Anthony Eden, Churchill's successor, is haunted by the years of appeasement in the Thirties. Nasser is another dictator who must be squashed and so secretly that summer Britain and France collude with Israel. The Israelis invade the Sinai Desert on October 30; Britain and France, proclaiming their aim as the protection of the Canal from both sides, bomb Cairo and on November 5 land troops at Port Said. The world is in tumult. Soviet tanks seize the moment to put down an anti-Communist uprising in Hungary and then threaten rocket attacks on London unless the British withdraw from Egypt. Eisenhower is furious with his former allies. Within days, Britain and France stop the invasion by which time the Suez Canal is blocked with scuttled ships. Things are never to be the same again. It is the real end of the imperial era, the beginning of domination by the United States and the Soviet Union. France drifts into Gaullism. Eden, a sick man, resigns the Premiership and Harold Macmillan takes over. In a grim year there is one piece of traditional progress. On September 26 electricity from nuclear power is produced for the first time at Marcoule in France.

The orphan of policy: anxiety and joy in a daughter's reunion with her father. Last of thousands of Germans kept as "prisoners of war" in Russia for 11 years after fighting stopped, he is home; but they are strangers. The Press Photograph of the Year, by H. R. Pirath

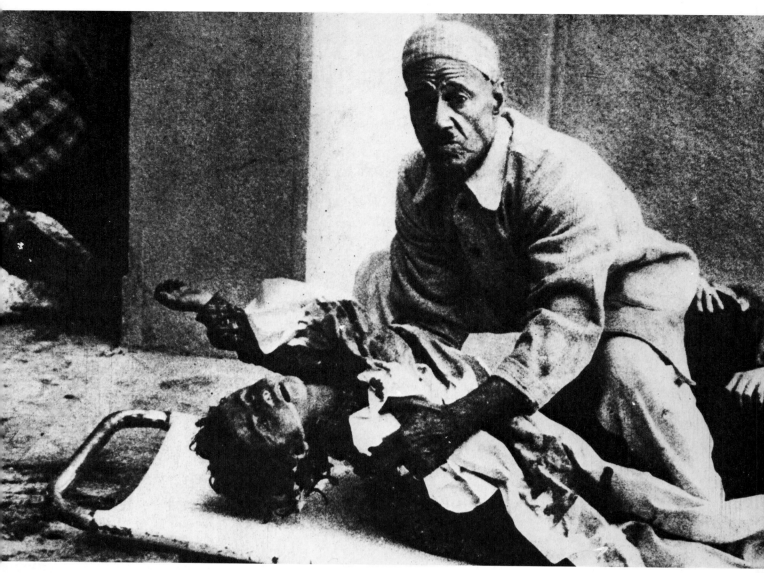

Suez: the man who started it (opposite page), Gamal Abdul Nasser; how it started (right): Israelis overwhelming an Egyptian position on the Canal; how it was conducted (centre): British troops evacuating wounded – those of the Egyptians as well as their own – for treatment in a Navy ship at Port Said; and (above) the man who paid for it with the life of his child, oblivious to national glory, to the sporting rules of war, to all but grief

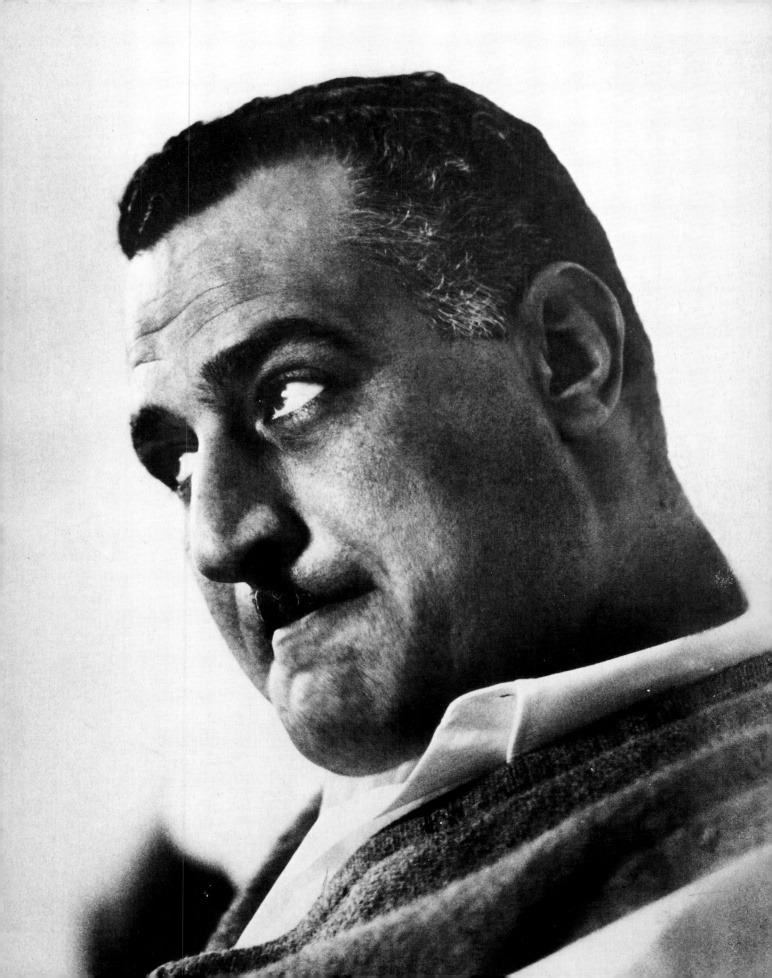

Revenge in Hungary: these men are security policemen in Budapest. More than 80 of them have been herded out of their headquarters into a courtyard by men who have joined the uprising and armed themselves. There they are summarily shot, without warning. Only the man in the centre, above, facing the camera, survives. Soon afterwards the Hungarian bid for freedom was crushed, with no less brutality, by troops and tanks of the USSR

1957: TOGETHERNESS

The New York Times.

PRESIDENT SENDS TROOPS TO LITTLE ROCK,
FEDERALIZES ARKANSAS NATIONAL GUARD;
TELLS NATION HE ACTED TO AVOID ANARCHY

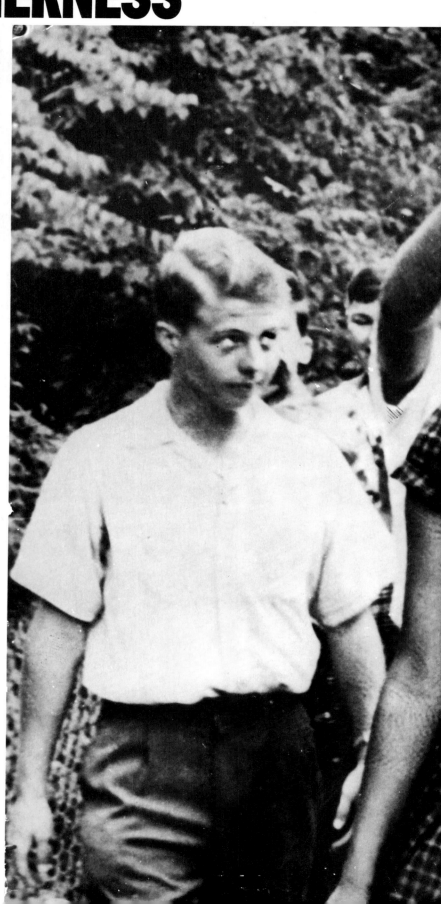

Nothing is ever to be the same after 1956 – and the events of 1957 show the world exactly where the differences are to lie after that watershed. Since 1949 Britain has remained aloof from the grindingly difficult diplomacy by which the western European states, led by France and Germany, reach towards unity. Still dazzled by a view of herself as a great imperial power, Britain rejects the offer of membership in the proposed European Economic Community. Six weeks later France, Germany, Italy, Holland, Belgium and Luxembourg sign the Treaty of Rome to bring the Common Market into being. Henceforward it is to be the dominant factor in European political life. By that time the first shadow of twilight already lies across the empire on which "the sun never sets": the Gold Coast is the first of Britain's possessions to become independent, as Ghana. In America, too, white dominance of blacks is showing the first fracture lines: three years after the Supreme Court's outlawing of racial segregation in schools, Eisenhower signs the Civil Rights Act and nine black students are admitted to Central High School in a hot centre of racial fission, Little Rock, Arkansas. Relying on "States rights" the governor, Orval Faubus, attempts to exclude the black students by force, setting off widespread disturbances. The President sends Federal troops to enforce the law against Faubus's National Guard. But within a week the world's attention to this skirmish is stunningly diverted: Russia bursts open the door into the new world of space by shooting an unmanned satellite into orbit round the Earth. The bleeping signals of Sputnik I, heard around the world, are the voice of the future.

Isolated among jeering whites, two of the first nine blacks admitted to Central High School, Little Rock, Arkansas, maintain an apprehensive dignity. Soon they will be at the centre of violent demonstrations, and the cause for which armed forces of "States rights" and Federal governments confront each other. The Press Photograph of the Year, by Douglas Martin

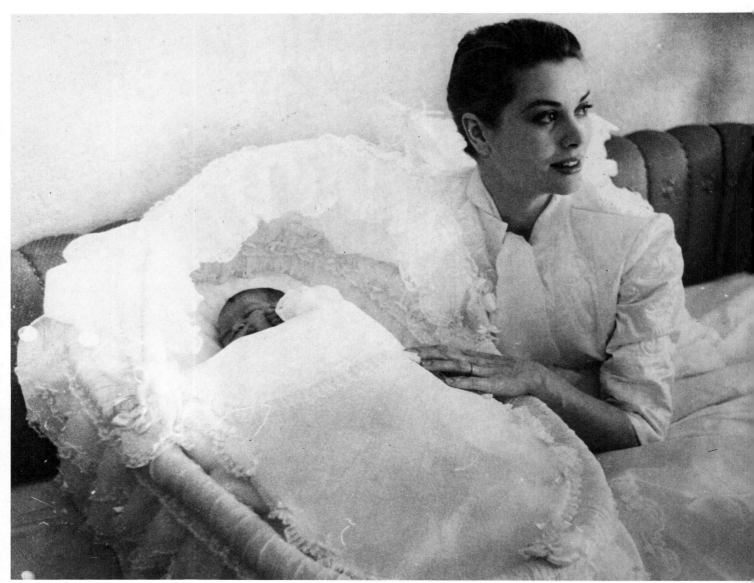

Birth of a princess: Princess Grace of Monaco (née Grace Kelly) poses at the cradle of her daughter Princess Caroline

Birth of a cinema queen: Sophia Loren going through the emotions for the camera, her constant courtier throughout her glorious reign

Chester Simpson, 16, walking through a Texas spring blizzard to see his girl, got lost: frozen to death, he is found only after the thaw

1958: GIANTS IN THOSE DAYS

The year of the coming of the giants – men who will dominate temporal and spiritual affairs well into the next decade and leave a changed world behind them. In the USSR Nikita Khrushchev assumes the premiership. In France, the impatience of the army and the growing violence of the nationalist struggle in Algeria bring about the fall of the Fourth Republic, whereupon General Charles de Gaulle is called from retirement to be Prime Minister. He frames the constitution of the Fifth Republic, wins the first of many referendums and an election to become President. He virtually scraps the French empire by announcing independence for all colonies: and those who saw him as the saviour of *Algérie française* begin to suspect they have been deceived. Half-way around the world Fidel Castro and his guerilla army have been making "total war" on the Cuban government under Fulgencio Batista; and on the last day of the year, he triumphs. Far away to the south, the dedicated architect of the grand design of *apartheid*, Dr Hendrik Verwoerd, succeeds to the premiership of the Union of South Africa. And in Latin America Dwight Eisenhower's relatively obscure Vice-President behaves with great courage in the face of violently hostile demonstrations. He is Richard Milhous Nixon. But there is something to set against these minatory spectres who will disturb the world's peace of mind for so long. After an agonisingly drawn-out election, white smoke from the Vatican chimney announces a successor to Pope Pius XII: Cardinal Roncalli, an old man whose physical ugliness is matched only by his spiritual beauty, takes the name John XXIII.

The end of the Havana Grand Prix, which had begun 15 minutes earlier without World Champion Fangio, who was "detained" by Castro's rebels. They were also accused of laying the oil patch on which Cifuentes's Ferrari skidded before ploughing into the crowd. After Castro's victory, there were no more Havana races

Little did the Venezuelan "students" know that they were helping to kick Richard Nixon upstairs: aggressive courage in the face of su

Soaker. Picture of the Year: Stanislav Tereba

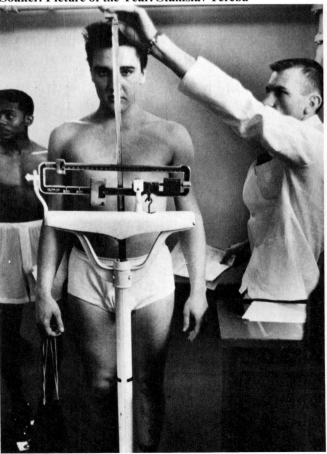

monstrations on his Latin American tour deeply impressed the Americans

Soldier king: Private Presley's army medical

1959: TRIUMPHS—BUT NOT MANY

On the threshold of a new decade, much of the world marks time, as if gathering its energies for what is to come. The exceptions are two island trouble spots: Cyprus, where Britain has been fighting an impossible small war to contain the EOKA movement for union with Greece, *enosis*; and Cuba, where on New Year's Day Fidel Castro marches victoriously through the capital from which Batista, the dictator of Cuba for seven years, has fled. In Cyprus, once independence is agreed, the Greek Cypriot leader, Archbishop Makarios, returns to a triumphal progress through Nicosia. In Havana Castro has enjoyed a similar reception. He appoints himself Prime Minister and at once begins a campaign to spread his revolution in Latin America and the Caribbean, only to meet successive failures in Panama, Dominica and Haiti. Meanwhile his drastic reforms in Cuba lead many of the middle-class to seek refuge in the U.S., where they constitute a time-bomb of resentment ready to be primed by American "hawks" seeking Castro's downfall. Britain, fearing the economic consequences of isolation from the EEC, agrees to form a rival economic grouping, the European Free Trade Association, with Austria, Denmark, Norway, Portugal, Sweden and Switzerland. A rising in Tibet is put down by the Chinese, and the Dalai Lama flees to India. Dr Verwoerd, the South African Prime Minister, outlines a scheme to provide "Bantustans" for blacks, excluding them from S.A. citizenship. In response, the UN General Assembly condemns *apartheid*. Khrushchev, leading his country's UN delegation, pays an official visit to the U.S.; and seems boastfully unimpressed by all he sees. A Russian spacecraft photographs the dark side of the moon; and Pope John summons the Second Vatican Council to promote church unity.

To a rapturous welcome from almost the entire Greek-Cypriot population, Archbishop Makarios returns to Nicosia from more than three years of exile at the hands of the British, who hoped to weaken the campaign for union with Greece. By the end of the year Cyprus is independent under President Makarios

Nikita Khrushchev, first Russian leader to visit U.S., confronts Lincoln; but he is not converted. Soon to be his ally, Castro (right) sets the style of his government

1960: LETHAL WINDS OF CHANGE

A year of terrible events and sombre omens. Two risings in Algeria are mercilessly repressed. Terrorism and counter-terrorism continue unabated. At the other end of the continent, Prime Minister Macmillan visits Central and South Africa, where he delivers a famous speech warning of the need to accept that "winds of change" are blowing through Africa. Soon after, South African police open fire on a gathering of blacks at Sharpeville, near Johannesburg, killing 67; for a time the country seethes on the brink of general violence and Prime Minister Verwoerd is shot and severely wounded as he addresses a rally. To the north the Belgian Congo, rushed into independence, explodes into a bloody chaos from which it will not recover for a decade. If less bloody, events in Europe are not less disturbing: in May an American U-2 spy plane is shot down over Russia, and the incident wrecks the Summit conference which follows in Paris. The "Cold War" intensifies. Israeli intelligence men kidnap Adolf Eichmann, sometime Gestapo chief, in South America and bring him to Israel for trial. Appeals for international policing from the Congo bring in UN troops – who cannot prevent the murder of Patrice Lumumba, first Congo premier, but achieve a temporary ceasefire; it is soon broken. There are many signs and portents, most of them unremarked: a woman becomes Prime Minister in Ceylon (Sri Lanka); East Germany begins a partial blockade of Berlin; and most ominous and unremarked of all, in Baghdad a group of oil producers sets up the Organisation of Petroleum Exporting Countries – OPEC. Outside America itself, the election as President there (by a vote margin of less than 0.2 per cent) of John Fitzgerald Kennedy is greeted with hardly less misgiving than if his opponent, Richard Nixon, had won.

The Belgians have given little to the Congo but names for its cities and a tradition of brutality which at once expresses itself in bloody chaos when they depart. Riots at Leopoldville, savagely suppressed, are the explosive precursor of years of continuous atrocity

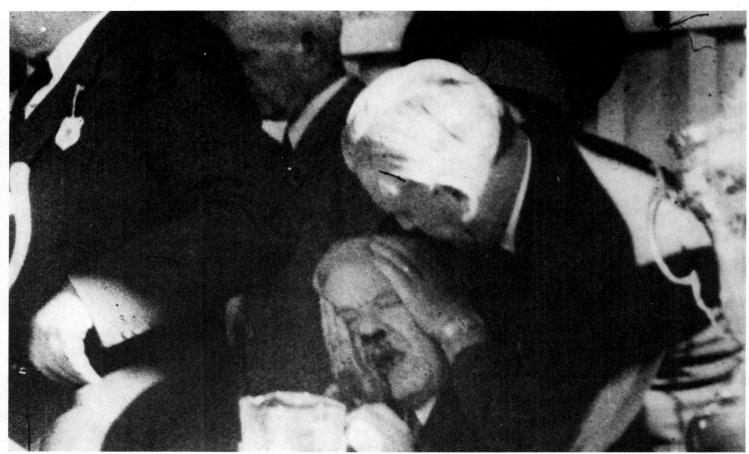

Three weeks after Sharpeville, South Africa's Premier Dr Verwoerd is shot and severely wounded by a white farmer. He recovers

Algiers: hints that de Gaulle will not risk all France to keep Algeria French encourage huge demonstrations. These are put down with customary severity. Right, a lone striker faces the troops in Belgium. Picture of the Year by Dolf Kruger

1961: WRITING ON THE WALL

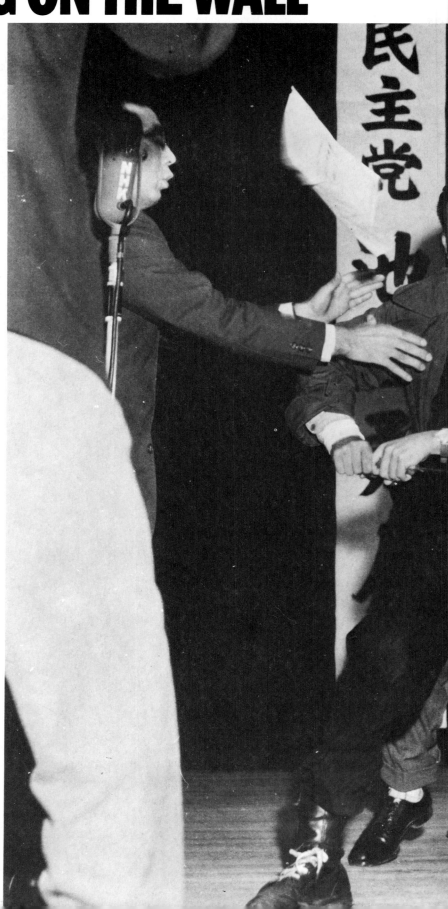

The public personality projected by John F. Kennedy as U.S. President in January is of such winning attractiveness that the world's misgivings evaporate: to be replaced by an extraordinary hopefulness, almost a belief, that this one youngish man will find a way to solve all problems. Yet with one exception the crucial events of the year take place in the Old World. The Algerian abscess finally comes to a head with the acceptance in a January referendum of de Gaulle's plans to give Algeria self-determination. A military revolt follows; is suppressed; and leads on to the formation by General Salan of the OAS, dedicated to keeping Algeria French and ousting de Gaulle. At the same time de Gaulle begins secret talks at Evian with the FLN. Later in the year the first of many attempts to assassinate him fails. President Kennedy inaugurates the U.S. Peace Corps, whose volunteers work in development schemes in the Third World. The USSR responds by putting Yuri Gagarin into a single orbit of the earth in the spacecraft *Vostok*. The best the U.S. can manage in reply is a short, non-orbital flight by Alan Shepherd. Between these essentially propagandist exercises, 1500 Cuban refugees, armed and drilled in the U.S. and encouraged by the CIA, are permitted by Kennedy to attempt an invasion of Cuba at the Bay of Pigs. The expected uprising against Castro fails to materialise: 1200 are captured, later to be ransomed. Kennedy's stock plummets, but it has been a valuable lesson. The British Empire continues to fragment. In May South Africa becomes a republic outside the Commonwealth; and all restrictions are removed from Jomo Kenyatta in Kenya. The UN Secretary-General, Dag Hammarskjöld, dies in a plane crash in the Congo. Around West Berlin, which they say acts as a drain for their population, the East Germans begin to build a security wall.

Hibiya Hall, Tokyo: Inejiro Asanuma, Chairman of the Socialist Party, addresses a rowdy meeting. Someone leaps on to the stage, and he turns to see who it is – in time to receive two fatal thrusts from a short sword in the hands of Otoya Yamaguchi, a right-wing student. The Picture of the Year, by Yasushi Nagao

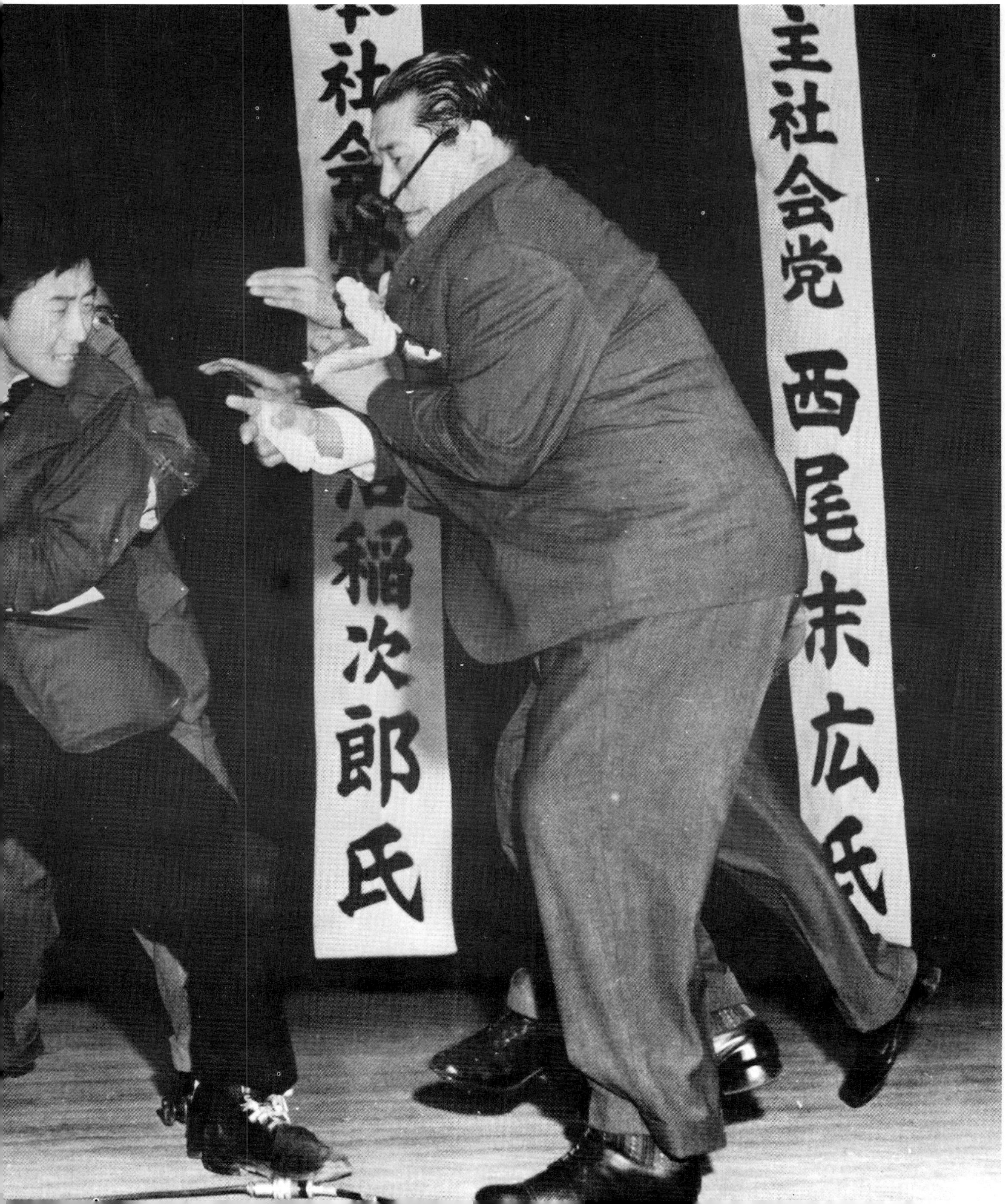
社会
稲次郎氏
主社会党
西尾末広氏

What all suburban householders fear – but it was the crew that was killed when this trainer came down on a rooftop in Gloucester, England. Right, the man in the glass box: Adolf Eichmann, kidnapped by Israelis in Latin America and put on trial, hears himself found guilty. Far right, Yuri Gagarin, the first human being to orbit the Earth, on his way to the launching pad where the *Vostok* is waiting. Opposite page: the first day of the Berlin Wall, and a young East German guard opens the new wire, against orders, for a child to get through

1962: TO THE BRINK

DAILY SKETCH **CUBA** SENSATIONAL MOVE BY KENNEDY

TUESDAY, OCTOBER 23, 1962 ... 36

© 1962, by the Daily Sketch

BLOCKADE!

Ultimatum to Kruschev
'Move those missiles'

PRESIDENT KENNEDY last night announced a full-scale blockade of Cuba to stop a build-up of Russian missiles there.

A year like any other; or so it seems while the focus of world attention remains in France, where independence for Algeria leads to an intensification of the campaign of violence in both countries by the OAS (*Organisation de l'Armée Secrète*) under General Salan: two unsuccessful attempts are made on de Gaulle's life. In the general relief, not much is made of the expulsion of Cuba from the other OAS (Organisation of American States) at U.S. instigation after a Russo-Cuban trade and arms pact. But, badly hurt by a U.S. trade embargo, Cuba turns to the USSR and announces that a Russian fishing base is to be built on the island. On October 22 Kennedy reveals – with photographic evidence – that the "fishing base" is designed to accommodate Russian medium-range missiles; and two days later mounts a naval blockade of Cuba to prevent the installation of the missiles already on their way, in a fleet of cargo ships, from Russia. The world holds its breath as Russian ships approach within hours of contact with the blockading fleet. Nuclear war seems inevitable. But at the last moment Khrushchev draws back from the abyss. His ships are ordered back and the installations in Cuba are dismantled. The astonishing hopes the world has invested in the Kennedy presidency seem magnificently justified: in the huge relief following the crisis he assumes a god-like status. Little else can be seen in proportion against the background of these climatic events – not the hanging of Adolf Eichmann in Israel; not the acceleration of the "space race", in which the U.S.'s three orbits with John Glenn are made to look puny by Nikolayev's 64 orbits for Russia; not even the arrival of the first American military "advisers" in far-off South Vietnam.

At the Puerto Cabello naval base in Venezuela, Fr Luis Padillo gazes at the sniper still trying to hit the mortally wounded soldier to whom the priest is giving final absolution, during a military rebellion. Picture of the Year by Hector Rondon Lovera

America is still well behind in the newly begun space race, soon after President Kennedy has publicly committed his country to reaching "the moon by the end of the decade". John Glenn (opposite page), America's first orbiting astronaut, manages three turns round the earth in his cramped capsule. A Russian soon does 64; but all is to change. Above: in Berlin the Wall has become part of the scenery, its lethal dramas already assimilated in the games of children nearby, after only one year. Left: "We have lift-off!"

1963: BAD NEWS

De Gaulle's bleak "Non" is enough to destroy British hopes of EEC membership; his will binds Europe together. But the eyes of the world are on Jack Kennedy, the Giant Killer, the flame of his personality brightened by the adulation of half the world, who in Berlin defies the Wall. "*Ich bin ein Berliner*," he proclaims as he reaffirms the essential unity of the West – even while the first rumblings of opposition are heard to the commitment of American fighting troops in support of South Vietnam. There, a Buddhist monk horrifyingly commits suicide in public by burning himself to death. Photographs of the event give a foretaste of how closely the whole world is to be involved in Vietnam's agony for the next decade or more. Little notice is taken of Southern Rhodesia's demand for independence, refused by Britain; where the Great Train Robbery (of £2.5 million) is treated with barely concealed admiration by all but the police. The spectacle of peers hurrying to renounce their titles to vie for the premiership given up by Macmillan diverts everybody: Lord Home wins, as Sir Alec Douglas Home. And that is the end of the fun. On November 22 John Kennedy is shot dead in Dallas. The grief of ruined hopes is piercingly felt all over an appalled world – which is not reassured by the sight of the supposed assassin being gunned down or by the suspicion that the truth has not been fully told. The Vice-President, Lyndon Baines Johnson, is sworn in. Pope John XXIII dies; his successor is an austerer man, Paul VI. The year, beginning in the worst winter in Europe for generations, ends everywhere in chilly apprehensiveness.

The news-hungry throng to Dallas jail to see Lee Harvey Oswald, accused killer of President Kennedy, taken to another prison two days after the assassination. From the crowd a night-club owner, Jack Ruby, takes three quick steps and – "Bang!": Oswald's face contorts as the bullet strikes him and he falls, dying, taking his secret with him

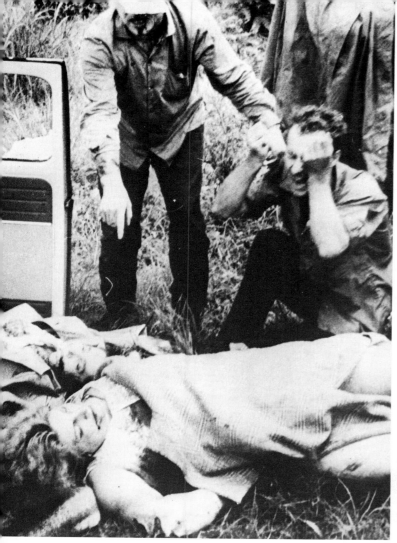

Soon after the death of President Kennedy his Vice-President, Lyndon B. Johnson, is sworn in as his replacement in the cabin of the presidential aircraft. With Johnson is Kennedy's wife Jacqueline (right). Meanwhile the Congo bloodbath continues: Albert Verbrugghe emerges wounded and screaming from his car after UN Indian troops open fire on him for failing to stop (opposite page). In the car his wife and a friend lie dead (above) and only his injured dog is left to comfort him as the peacekeepers move on again

Light relief: Indonesia's Soekarno jokingly picks minister's pocket

Picture of the Year: Buddhist suicide, Saigon; Malcolm Brown

Birmingham, Alabama, where police use dogs to break up a black civil rights demonstration; and a young woman prays for its success

A weeping father carries his dead baby through the streets of Skopje, Yugoslavia, where in July an earthquake killed more than 1000

46

1964: COMMITMENTS

This is the year in which people embark on or settle into courses of action which will occupy them, and the world, for many years to come. In Cyprus Greeks and Turks begin the fighting which is only to end in partition of the island more than a decade hence. Britain fulfils almost her last commitment in Africa by providing troops to put down army mutinies in Tanganyika and Kenya – but not quite the last: Rhodesia, the remaining British colony of the defunct Central African Federation (Zambia and Malawi having been made out of Northern Rhodesia and Nyasaland) shows signs of rebellion under its new Prime Minister Ian Smith. He is warned to tread carefully by another new Prime Minister, Harold Wilson, who brings 13 years of Conservative rule to an end in Britain with a majority in the House of Commons of four for his Labour Party. He brings a new style to British politics that is to dominate them, in and out of office, for the next decade: he changes the emphasis of public spending on industry; and begins the growth of trade union power that is to become the main feature of British economic life. In America, in pursuit of dead President Kennedy's space-race legacy ("a man on the moon by the end of the decade"), NASA shoots a spacecraft to the moon to photograph every part of it. Elsewhere in the U.S. there are riots by blacks after the passage of the Civil Rights Act: henceforth Americans will greet the "long, hot summer" with apprehension. Fresh from a landslide re-election victory, President Johnson is newly committed to the U.S.'s war in Vietnam after an attack on U.S. ships in the Gulf of Tonkin. Frustrated by the refusal of Israel to yield to pressures, an Arab summit conference in Cairo sets up the Palestine Liberation Organisation, with a brief to use any means towards the achievement of a Palestinian state.

A Turkish child reaches out to his newly-widowed mother, as much to give as to demand comfort, after fighting between Greeks and Turks near her Cyprus village. Picture of the Year by Donald McCullin

Top: a farmer in South Vietnam is thought not to have told all he knows; a Ranger uses the butt of his knife to extract the last bit. Above, earthquake in Alaska. Right, Russia: life on the tundra at 50°C below zero

1965: BROKEN LINKS

In the new year Sir Winston Churchill dies. Vast crowds line the streets for his state funeral. But his contemporary, Dr Albert Schweitzer, dies at Lambarène almost unnoticed, a relic of the colonial past. That past is not so easily escaped from: in one of Britain's surviving colonies the Prime Minister, emboldened by overwhelming victory at the polls, makes a unilateral declaration of independence. Rebellious Rhodesia is treated with some indulgence at first, and no-one can foresee that it will defy for 14 years the efforts of Britain, the United Nations and the guerilla armies of its own black majority to restore it to legality. Its symbolic importance exceeds, in the black Third World, even that of Vietnam; where the war between North and U.S.-assisted South enters a new phase with the bombing of the North by the U.S. In America, where President Johnson has called upon the people to build the "Great Society", the war is far from universally popular; there are demonstrations against U.S. involvement. The huge resources made available to the U.S. space programme begin to show results; an unmanned spacecraft is landed on the moon; and Edward White becomes the first man to leave a spacecraft and "walk" in space. American blacks, more impressed by the failure of some southern states to grant them civil rights, continue to march in protest. The Nobel Peace Prize winner Dr Martin Luther King is arrested, twice; and a leader of different style, "Malcolm X" of the Black Muslims, is assassinated. Even in "Swinging London", intent on having a good time, there seems not much to be optimistic about.

He is still known by the name of a famous white man. But tonight the white man's existence is forgotten: Cassius Clay is black, Heavyweight Champion of the World, perhaps the greatest ever, and has finished off his challenger, ex-Champion Sonny Liston, in 60secs

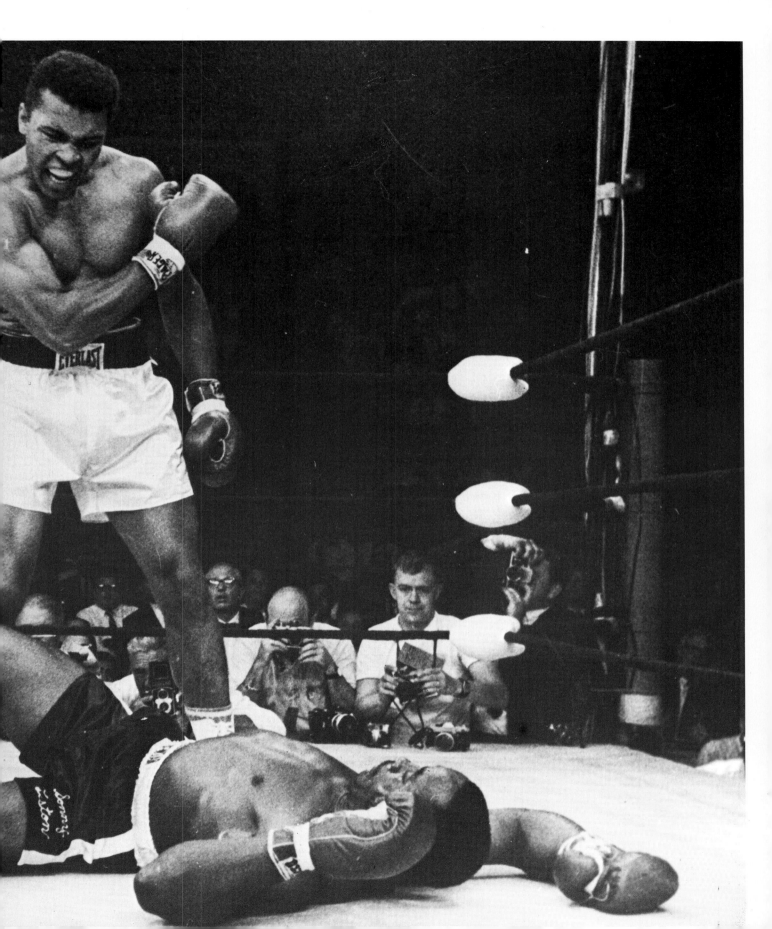

Vietnam, where the war intensifies and the American presence has grown to almost 200,000 troops – some of whom have just been bombing the village from which this woman wades to safety across the river, her children clutched about her. Yesterday the Vietcong used the village as a base, today it no longer exists. Picture of the Year by Kyoichi Sawada. Right, fire breaks out in a mosque; spectators gather to watch as its fabric is eaten by the flames – and run in panic as it majestically kills itself. Opposite page: U.S. police demonstrate how necessary was the protesting placard they have confiscated, along with a little U.S. flag symbolising the values they strike down

1966: RISES AND FALLS

The ferocity and scale of the war in Vietnam increase. Now there are many photographers and reporters assigned to the war, and many television crews: the horrors being suffered and inflicted by their fellow-countrymen are seen in detail by millions of Americans. Their outrage becomes a significant factor in the conduct of the war. In Africa it is a year of fallen leaders and seized governments: Bokassa takes power in the Central African Republic, there is an Ibo *coup d'état* in Nigeria which brings General Ironsi to power only to be ejected in a counter-*coup* under Col. Gowon, Obote overthrows the Uganda constitution and in Ghana a military government takes over while Kwame Nkrumah is out of the country. In Cape Town the second attempt to assassinate Dr Verwoerd succeeds as he sits in his own Parliament: his killer is said to be deranged. John Vorster succeeds to the leadership of Afrikanerdom. The Indian Prime Minister, Lal Bahadur Shastri, dies suddenly while visiting Tashkent; and Mrs Indira Ghandi becomes the world's second woman Prime Minister. Mao Tse Tung launches a ''cultural revolution'' to purge the Chinese of their past – including any friendship for the USSR, against whom an alliance with Albania is signed. The West's own alliance, NATO, suffers two setbacks: Spain forbids overflying after the U.S. loses a hydrogen bomb there in an accident; and General de Gaulle, hostile to American influence, withdraws from the organisation and forbids his country's soil to U.S. troops. This does not deter Britain from once again seeking membership of the EEC; but the stubborn deviousness of Ian Smith defeats Prime Minister Wilson's first attempt, aboard HMS *Tiger*, to bring Rhodesia back to legality by personal diplomacy. There is no more talk of the rebellion lasting ''weeks rather than months''.

Bao Trai, Vietnam: when a South Vietnam sweep is held up by North Vietnamese snipers and grim-faced men with grenade launchers arrive in their village, the ordinary Vietnamese know what to do – take cover, even if it means sitting half-submerged in the canal

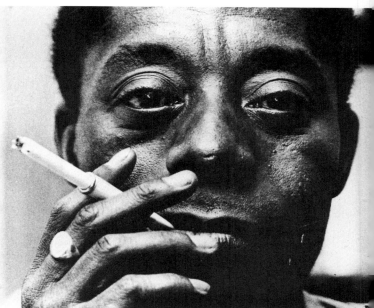

Top: another sniper in Texas, this time in Austin, where Charles Whitman takes out his grudge against the world with a rifle from a high building, shooting indiscriminately into the crowds below him. Near one of his victims, while his bullets spatter the pavement, a terrified young woman cowers behind a statue. Above, two handed public relations. President Johnson and his Vice-President, Hubert Humphrey, share the heavy work of shaking hundreds of well-wishing hands. Above right, a portrait of the black writer James Baldwin. Opposite page, the scene at Aberfan, a mining village in South Wales, after a new colliery tip turned to mud and slid remorselessly through the local school and many houses, killing 144 people of whom 116 were young children

1967: APOCALYPSE NOW

Of the Four Horsemen only Pestilence is missing from this year. War and Famine and Death are much in evidence. There are violent riots in Aden against the British. In Greece a *junta* of colonels lead a military coup and later banish their king to Rome. In Nigeria the new government of General Gowon organises the federation into 12 states – and the whole oil-rich Eastern Region, homeland of the Ibos, secedes under Col. Ojukwu, calling itself by the ancient name of Biafra. Civil war begins, Biafra is blockaded and begins to starve. Almost immediately there is trouble in the Middle East, where Egypt decides to deny the Gulf of Aqaba to Israel. Tension mounts and, on June 5, the Israelis launch what becomes known as the Six Day War, so rapid and devastatingly successful is their campaign. In America the "Long, Hot Summer" begins with race riots in Florida which are repeated in many U.S. cities until it seems that disorder will engulf the country. There seems a likelihood that disturbances may also break out in Canada, where separatists in Quebec are brought to a state of frenzy by an inflammatory speech from de Gaulle ("*Vive le Québec libre!*") on a visit to the province. The visit is cut short. As President Johnson outlines proposals for peace in Vietnam, one of the most troublesome enemies of American influence in Latin America, Che Guevara, Castro's right hand, is caught and shot by troops in Bolivia. Near Christmas Dr Christiaan Barnard in South Africa performs the first human heart transplant, from a newly-dead mixed-race man to a Mr Waschansky, a white. Nearer still, as a celebration of Franco-British co-operation, the first supersonic Concorde flies from Toulouse; but General de Gaulle at once vetoes an EEC agreement to admit Britain to Europe.

President Nasser has blockaded the Israeli Red Sea port of Eilat; the Israeli response is a devastatingly quick and destructive *blitzkrieg* which brings Egypt to her knees in days. Now, as Israeli armour moves up to the Canal, stripped and bewildered Egyptian prisoners of war are taken in lorry-loads to the rear

The war of the year takes six days from beginning
to end – but there is another war, of every year
anybody under 30 can remember. Near Con Thien
in South Vietnam a U.S. Marine, bandaged and
bloodied, digs painfully deeper to hide himself from
North Vietnamese mortar fire (above). Elsewhere in
the same country one of the Russian ground-to-air
missiles the Vietcong are learning to use proves its
effectiveness: a U.S. plane falls broken from the
sky (right). To the intense stress of simply keeping
alive in battle, modern warfare adds the need to
concentrate on keeping high-technology equipment
functioning: and it shows on the face of this
U.S. tank commander in Vietnam. This is WPP's
Photograph of the Year, by Co Rentmeester

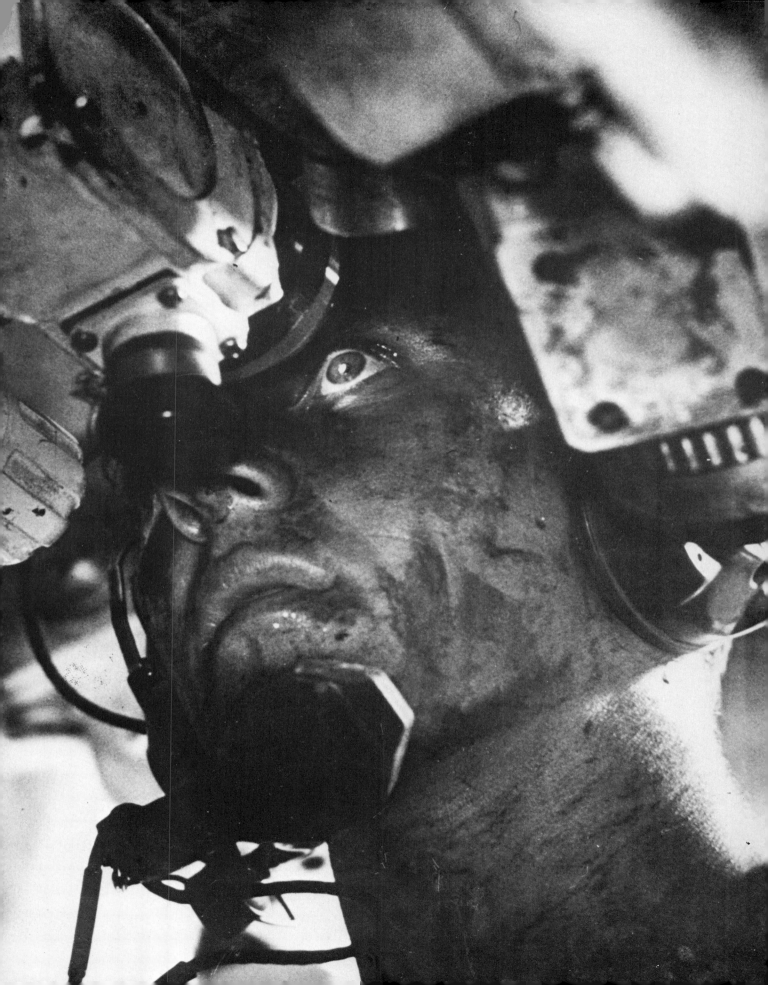

1968: CRACKS IN THE PAVING

Governments everywhere feel the foundations shift beneath them. At the beginning of a momentous year Alexander Dubcek is elected First Secretary of the Czech Communist Party, and immediately sets about a programme of liberal reforms – "Socialism with a human face". Czechoslovaks' exhilaration in the "Prague Spring" is so intense that its vibrations can be felt throughout Europe. In Moscow there is alarm – so much that in high summer the Soviet tanks roll by night over the Czech border and impose conformity. In Paris in May student riots spread until the streets of the Left Bank are in continual violent turmoil. Serious strikes follow. There are many to say that a revolution is succeeding. Yet amid these *événements de mai* a general election takes place in which Gaullists win 72 per cent of the seats. By summer, it is all over; but the Vietnamese peace talks, beginning in Paris, are to continue for five years. America has other Asian problems, too: the year is spent trying to extract the seized spy-ship Pueblo from the North Koreans. A tremor of fear for the safety of the Union passes through the U.S. as first Martin Luther King and then, nine weeks later, Senator Robert Kennedy, are removed by assassins' bullets. Kennedy's death leaves the Democrats without a strong presidential candidate: in November the Republicans' nominee wins handsomely. He is Richard Nixon. In Northern Ireland civil rights riots usher in the endless emergency. And in Rhodesia the first shots are fired in the 10-year guerilla war for majority rule. The longest-lived dictator, Dr Salazar, gives up the ghost in Portugal: his successor, Caetano, does not seem as tough.

A prisoner, identified as a Vietcong officer in Saigon, is taken to police chief Nguyen Ngoc Loan, who shoots him out of hand: the instant of his death, seen by so many in their newspapers, becomes the instant when Western opinion about the Vietnam war shifts fundamentally. Picture of the Year by Eddie Adams

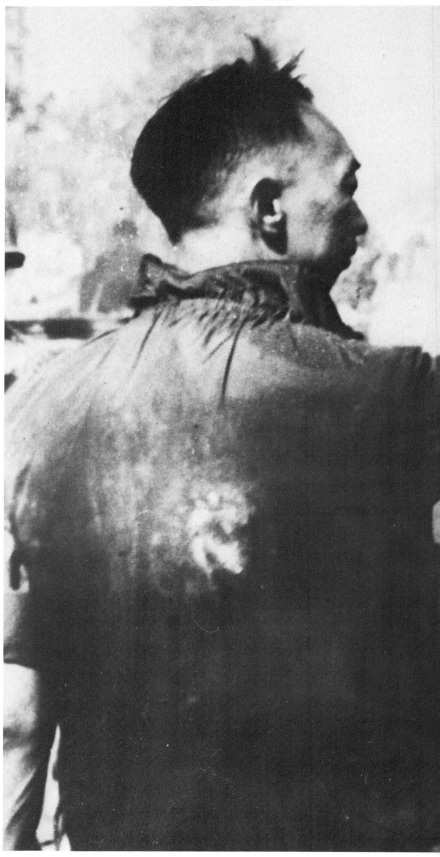

The spy ship Pueblo, sent by the U.S. to Korean waters, has been captured by North Koreans and kept for almost a year: now the crew are released to return home, where the captain, Lloyd Bucher, is greeted by his wife and sons (above). In Europe an old story is repeating itself: the USSR cannot let Czechoslovakia, any more than Hungary, crack the monolith of Warsaw Pact discipline. The "Prague Spring" comes to an end under the guns of Russian tanks in spite of incidents like this one. And in the U.S., too, it is as if history is being re-run: Robert Kennedy, while he campaigns to become the Democrats' presidential candidate, is assassinated at a meeting in a hotel by a lone gunman (opposite page)

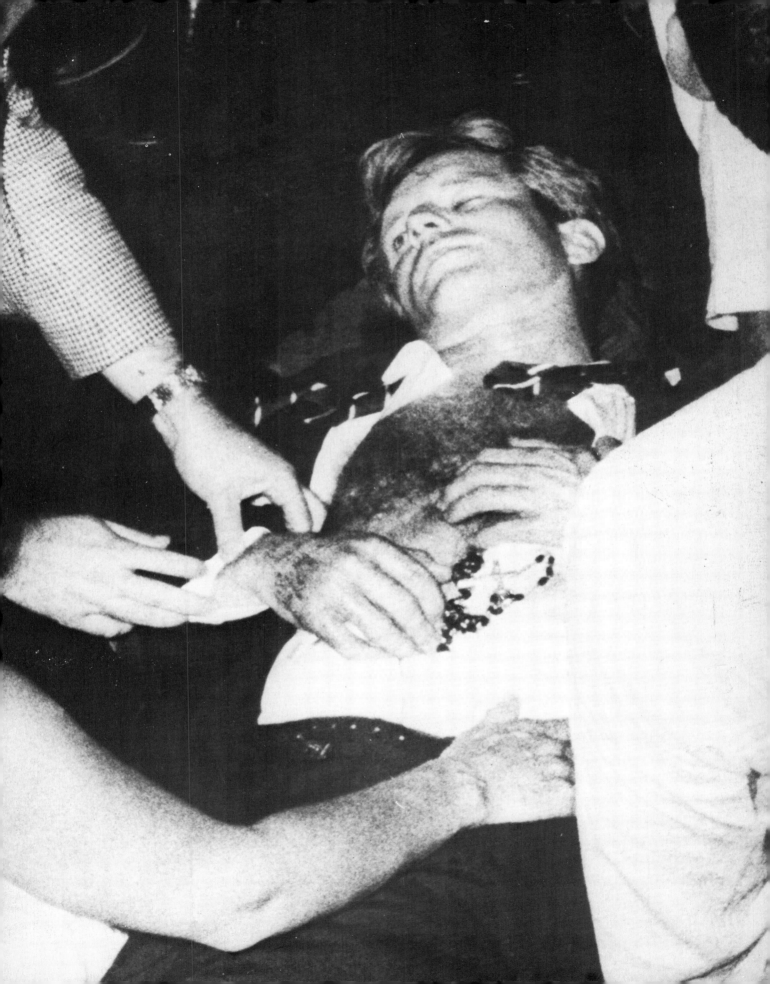

1969: GIANT STEPS

Gambling on a referendum, General de Gaulle is rejected by the people and goes at once. It is a petulantly tame ending to the striding reign of the colossus. His successor, Georges Pompidou, is ready to be kinder to a British application for EEC membership. There are more disturbances in Northern Ireland and the army is called in, at first in a small way. Uganda, at a Commonwealth Conference, announces a shorter way with troublesome minorities: 40,000 Asians are simply to be expelled. Ho Chi Minh, President of North Vietnam, dies, having already rejected the first U.S. peace proposals: this does not prevent anti-war demonstrators in America from chanting his name as they march. Their conviction is bolstered by the revelation of a massacre at My Lai the previous year, perpetrated by U.S. troops under Lieutenant William Calley, who is charged with murder. Israel elects to follow the trend set by Sri Lanka and India and installs Mrs Golda Meir as Prime Minister. The first use of diplomatic kidnapping as a guerilla weapon occurs in Brazil, where the U.S. Ambassador is bartered for 15 political prisoners. The spectacle of the decade is presented in July: America puts two men on the Moon, where they walk, jump, take photographs, exclaim and sleep before taking off and triumphantly returning to Earth. "A small step for man," says Neil Armstrong, as he becomes the first human being ever to set foot on a world in space, "but a giant leap for mankind," It is not great oratory: but it will serve. And there are very few to disagree with the judgment, or to cavil at this up-beat ending to a decade in which Earth's music has become ever more sombre and discordant.

Inside the ungainly Michelin-man with its enormous back-pack and clumsy boots is a real man; and he is the focus of the decade's most extraordinary feat of organisation and technology. He is Neil Armstrong; and he is the first human being to stand on the moon

The perils of protest: above, Japanese students have been
demonstrating in Kyoto. Many petrol-bombs have already been
thrown at police - and then one goes wrong for the thrower: he
and a comrade are drenched in burning petrol and run blazing
and helpless through the streets. Opposite page, at the Hague a
"human rights" demonstration by Antilleans turns, for this one
man, into an unequal race between himself and the menacing
horses with their stick-wielding riders. Right, the mourning
Mamie Eisenhower beside the coffin of "Ike", great wartime
commander and U.S. President during the Fifties. Opposite
page below, Belfast, where this year the pious slogan on the wall
begins to look like a bad joke as "civil rights" demonstrators –
mainly from the Catholic community – and "loyalists" –
mainly Protestant – clash with terrible ferocity. "The
Troubles" begin. Picture of the Year by Hans-Jörg Anders

1970: GUERILLA TACTICS

After two years during which the world has watched aghast as famine has harrowed Biafra, the war comes to an end. The land is littered with skeletal children listlessly awaiting death or succour. But victorious Nigerian troops behave with forbearance and there is at last some hope of preventing the passive destruction of the Ibo by starvation. Another Middle East war appears to be beginning between Israel and Syria, but both sides draw back in time. No such inhibitions influence the U.S. and South Vietnam forces, which attack Cambodia to cut Vietcong supply lines. Student protests about this lead, at Kent State University, to 13 students being shot by National Guardsmen, four fatally. The death roll is substantially higher in Jordan, where Palestinian guerillas fight, and are suppressed by, the Jordanian army; the incident becomes known as "Black September" and gives its name to the most ruthless of the guerilla groups. PLO techniques to gain publicity for their cause now centre on plane hijackings, after a try-out in 1969: there are five this year. Elsewhere guerillas make diplomacy a hazardous occupation: many diplomats are kidnapped and four are murdered. In Chile, Salvador Allende, a marxist, is elected President. In Britain the Conservatives take office; and almost immediately Britain, Norway, Denmark and Ireland formally apply for EEC membership. No one will say "Non": de Gaulle has died. President Nasser dies, unsettling the Middle East. Oil is found beneath the North Sea, but at $2.50 a barrel its exploitation is barely economic.

Biafra has collapsed; the civil war is over; but for Ibo children and their mothers the appalling misery goes on as famine still stalks the land. At last it is possible to get supplies through – but can they arrive in time?

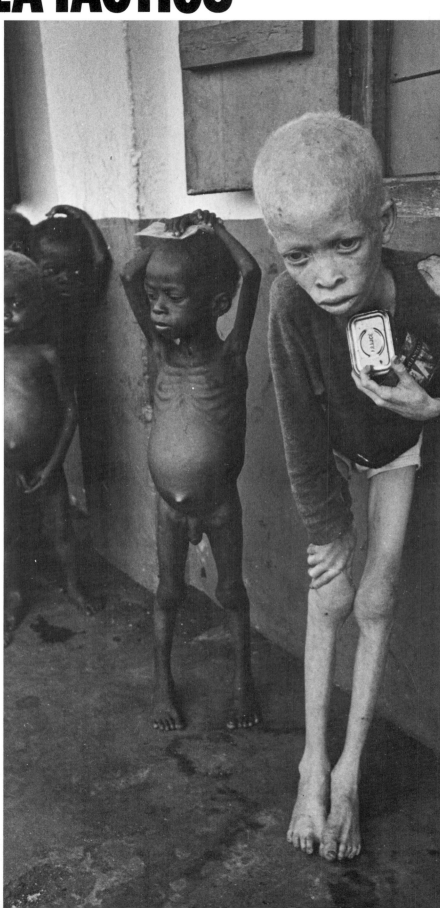

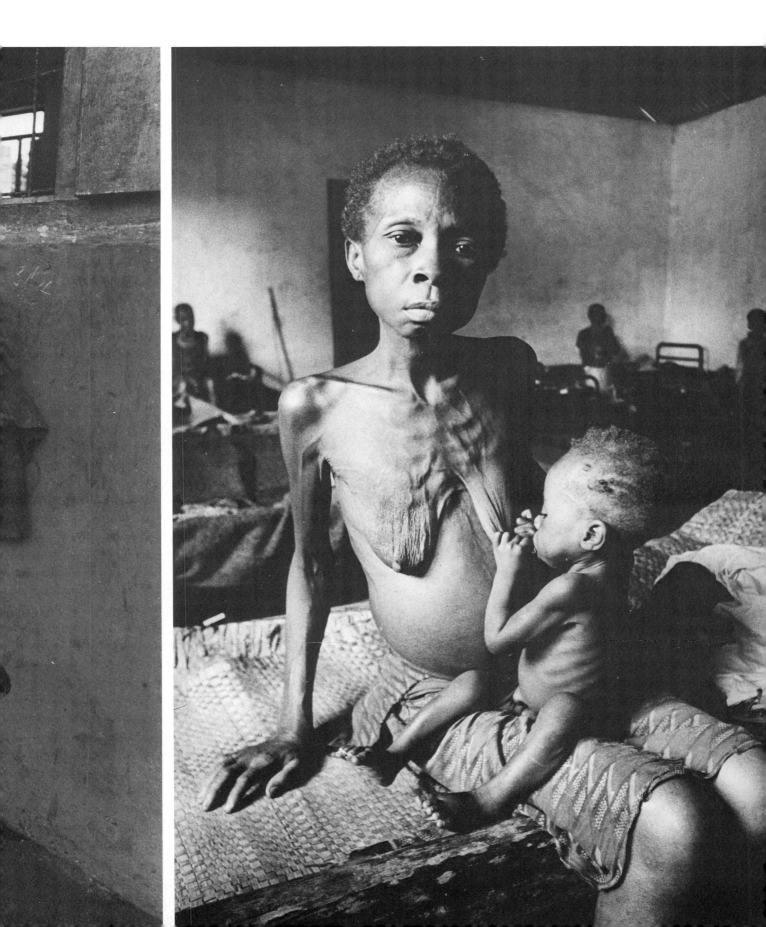

Little wars, big wars: a 10-year-old is not thought too young to join the rioting in Londonderry or, if his petrol-bomb finds its target, to burn someone to death for not being of the right religion (opposite page). In the big war American gunship crews can be jubilantly confident of ultimate victory – but it will always escape them (above). And in Biafra the commanders are preparing to continue to fight, as guerillas

The penalties of opposition
to established authority vary –
and not necessarily according
to whether you are violent or not.
For some protestors, it is just
a matter of being walked all over,
in a good-humoured way. For
some, like the protester above,
it is a gauntlet run between
grinning policemen with sticks.
But for others it is clubs
and guns, like the Black Panthers
(opposite, below); or sudden
death because soldiers lose their
tempers, as at Kent State
University (right), where four
unarmed students died

Divisions are not always clear-cut, even between Palestinians and Israelis. This girl is Leila Khaled, a heroine to the PLO but a villainess from the point of view of various authorities: she is the leader of a hi-jack gang which does not succeed but leads to more hi-jackings which do. Opposite is one of the people the PLO would like to believe do not exist: he is an Arab who fights for his country, Israel

1971: NATIONAL CHARACTER

For: 76 Against: 35 **CHINA IS VOTED INTO THE UN**
Singing and sadness

SINGING in the aisles at the United Nations . . . . gloom in Taiwan and in Washington . . . . hurried revaluations of policy all over the world.

Does President Nixon announce an end to U.S. offensives in Vietnam because of the great protest march of 200,000 people on Washington? Or as a gesture to the Chinese, recently admitted to the UN and the target for 1972 of a Nixon visit? Or because he is already thinking of the election of 1972? There is light, at any rate, at the end of the Vietnam tunnel. Not that the world has nothing else to worry about: East Pakistan becomes Bangladesh on the declaration of Shaikh Mujibur Rahman, and is plunged into fighting, epidemic cholera and general chaos; deaths are put at three million. The remainder of Pakistan goes to war with India and is defeated: General Yahya Khan resigns and Zulfikar Bhutto takes his place as Prime Minister. In Uganda Sgt Idi Amin takes over (promoting himself General) while Milton Obote's back is turned: some people think he is a joke, but Britain will find his refugees a serious matter. The EEC agrees to UK entry; and the House of Commons endorses the agreement by a substantial majority. The first British soldier is killed in the current Northern Ireland troubles; Rolls-Royce, a name to conjure with, can no longer turn a trick and goes broke; and on top of all, decimal currency is introduced to bewilder the populace – not by its strangeness but by the alarming inflation it seems to foster. The oil exporting nations tentatively flex their muscles and the price of crude goes up by 30 cents a barrel: oil companies consider this "ruinous". Most people are more alarmed by the Latin American kidnapping spree, and much relieved when the Tupamaros release Geoffrey Jackson, British ambassador to Uruguay, after nine months of imprisonment. U Thant escapes from the UN Secretary-Generalship; and Kurt Waldheim accepts the poisoned chalice. And a U.S. ping-pong team paves the way in China for President Nixon: they lose, perhaps diplomatically.

For 22 years China, most populous nation on earth, has been unrepresented at the U.N., since "China's" membership stayed with the regime of the defeated Chiang Kai Shek, based on Taiwan. Now America's attitude softens: China is admitted, Taiwan expelled

Bangladesh is born in blood and loses perhaps three million in fighting and a cholera epidemic: feelings run high against any man suspected of having been on the side of the Pakistanis in the struggle for independence. But can anything excuse the gleeful sadism of the torture and killing of these men, on a polo field – it seems for sport as much as revenge? It is a slur on the claims of the new state; and another terrible proof of the horrors of which all men seem to be capable

A fine new concrete bridge has been constructed across
a South African river and the old girder bridge which has for
so many years served there has to be demolished. It is
a routine task – except that the dying bridge takes revenge
on its attackers: as a span collapses cables knock the
white foreman and a black worker (just about to fall from the
left side of the bridge pier in this picture) into the
river. Both are lost. Opposite page: fire gains a hold with
such terrible speed at the Tae Yun Kak hotel in Seoul
that there can be no hope of rescue for people inside before
they are burned – and some of them are driven to leap
from windows clutching mattresses, hoping they will cushion
the long fall. All those who jump are killed. Right:
a bawling-out for one of the shaven-headed U.S. Marine
trainees undergoing the rigours of the notorious course
at Parris Island, South Carolina, where no-one "stands easy"

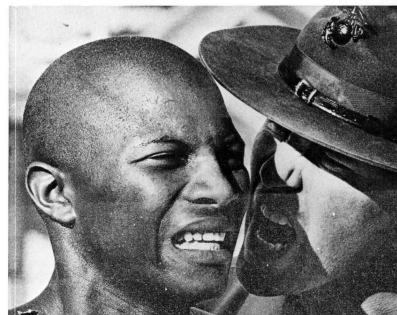

The pursuit of three bank-robbers ends near the West German town of Saarbrücken: the leader of the robbers, Kurt Vicenik, walks up to the police to negotiate a safe-conduct (the gang holds a hostage). Almost at once the leading policeman draws a gun and shoots him. The rest of the gang open fire and policemen run for cover while the photographers stand firm. The other two men are captured in the fight. Vicenik is dead. Pictures of the Year, by W.P. Geller

1972: DIRTY TRICKS

Northern Ireland, until now a "local difficulty" suddenly assumes international status as a hot-spot: British soldiers shoot 13 demonstrators dead in Londonderry on "Bloody Sunday", January 30. In Ireland a mob burns the British embassy; and in Aldershot the IRA revenge themselves with a bomb that kills seven. Direct rule from London is instituted. In West Germany the Olympic Games go off with the appearance of international harmony – until Israeli athletes are kidnapped and held hostage by "Black September" Palestinian guerillas: a shoot-out leaves 11 athletes, five guerillas and a policeman dead. In the U.S. presidential election campaign Governor George Wallace of Alabama is shot by a would-be assassin and crippled, President Nixon visits Moscow and Peking and warms to the Chinese, the Vietnam peace talks reach tentative agreement and there is only some trifling carping about a burglary at the Democratic Party headquarters, in a building called the Watergate, to take the gloss off Nixon's stunning Republican victory in November. There is a *rapprochement*, after 22 chilly years, between Britain and China; but Pakistan leaves the Commonwealth, offended over the Bangladesh issue. General (shortly Field-Marshal) Amin deports 8000 Ugandan Asians. Britain resettles them while conducting a "Cod war" with Iceland, which has closed traditional trawling grounds to outsiders. A peace commission in Rhodesia fails; and the only comfortable news for the West is that Egypt has asked 20,000 Russian military advisers to go. But Australians repose as much hope in their new government under Gough Whitlam's Labour Party as the British did when Harold Wilson took office. Time will tell.

What napalm does, even when it does not kill: children run crying down a Vietnam road from the holocaust of their village. Phan Thi Kim Phuc is nine, and naked because she has torn off her flaming clothing, and she is screaming and screaming because she is in pain as well as mortal terror. Picture of the Year: Huynh Cong Ut

Opposite page: the crippled Governor George Wallace of Alabama, shot by a would-be assassin during the earlier campaign, on the platform at the Democratic Convention to choose the Democrats' presidential candidate. Tough fighter though he is, his hopes of the presidency are over. Left: the candidate the Democrats choose, George McGovern, is simply swamped by the re-election machine of the President, Richard Nixon, whose wife winks at the running-mate and future Vice-President, Spiro Agnew, at the Republicans' Convention. So far, there is no mention of Watergate, which is still just the name of a Washington apartment building. Above: being President means sending men like Kenneth James Frazier to bomb North Vietnam – and to be shot down and put on public display by the Vietcong

The end of U.S. offensives in Vietnam means that the South Vietnamese now have to undertake the burden of their nightmare war

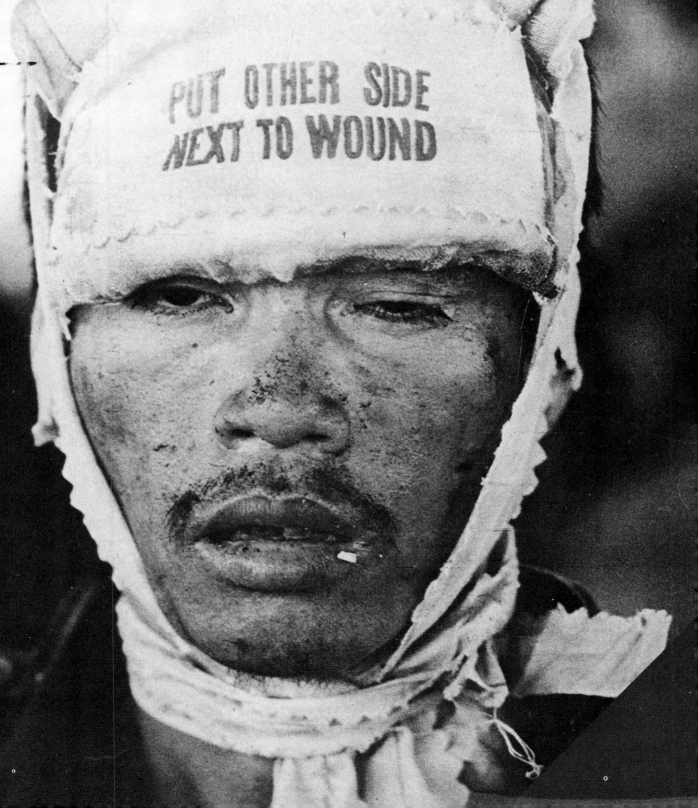

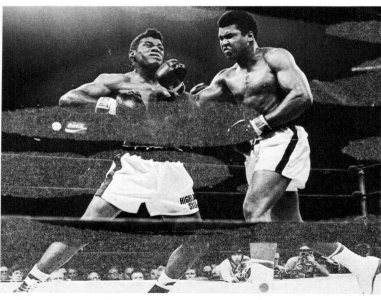

The Olympic Games take place at Munich and provide a fortnight of spectacle and excitement – and a shattering and tragic climax as 11 of the Israeli contingent die at the hands of their kidnappers. The Games themselves are dominated by American Mark Spitz, who breaks most of the records available to freestyle swimmers and takes seven gold medals – another record. No knowing how much the big man weighs (top), but his opponent looks in serious danger – as does Muhammad Ali's, Floyd Patterson (above)

Royalty slightly losing its dignity (above): the Queen of England, watching elephants in Thailand, is taken from behind. Opposite: almost-royalty in grief, putting on a chilling dignity – the Duchess of Windsor mourns her husband, sometime King Edward VIII, who gave up a throne for her. Right: faithful beyond death, a dog which refuses to leave the body of its friend, car-killed

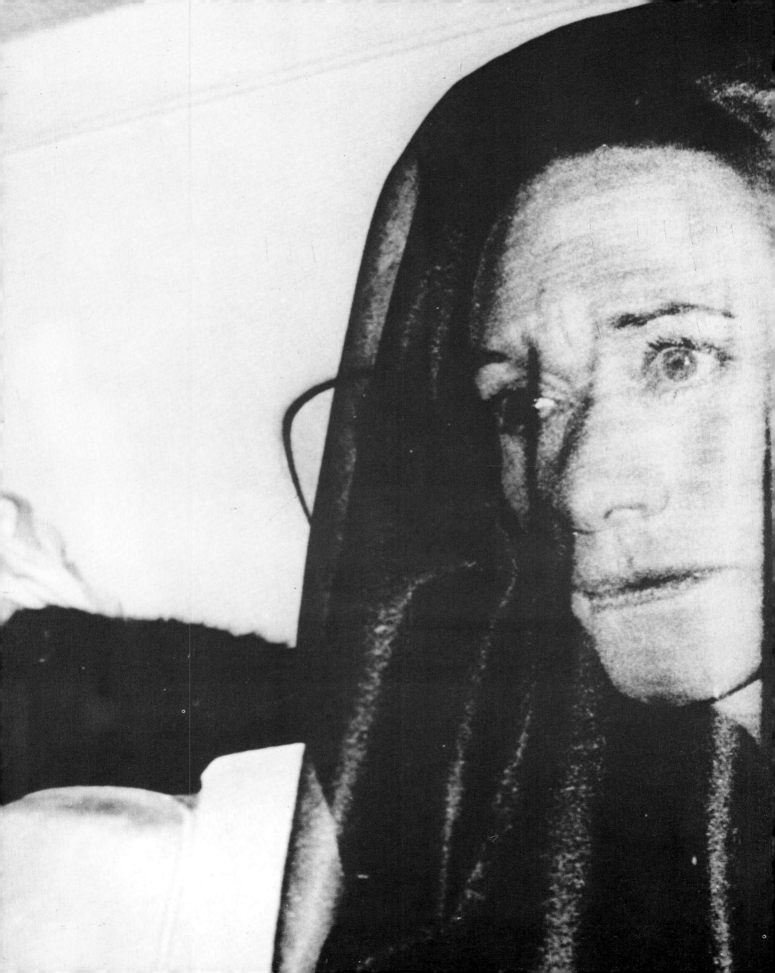

CLOSING STOCK PRICES
Pages 57-59

New York Post

FINAL

WATERGATE

- **Guard White House Files**
- **Senate Asks New Prober**
- **Ehrlichman Knew About The Ellsberg Burglary**

"All shook up" Elvis Presley used to sing. This year it is the world's theme song. The economic supremacy of the rich north is broken. The endless Vietnam war is over. The unbounded respect Americans have for their Presidents evaporates in a cloud of lies. Only in Argentina does it look as if the clock has turned back: Juan Perón returns to the Presidency from his years of exile. On New Year's Day Britain, Denmark and Eire accede to the EEC: now all the old enemies are in the same boat. There are fears, about prices, as well as hopes, about the embracing of people of common heritage and the end of European wars. In America there is rejoicing at the end of the foreign war that has sapped the Union's confidence and solidarity. The rejoicing fades as newspapers uncover details of the Watergate break-in and the links between it and the President. There is talk of his impeachment. In Chile, President Allende is overthrown in a military *coup* and dies – either by suicide or murder, depending on who is reporting the death. Change and decay are seen all around – although when an Arab-Israeli war breaks out in October, at Yom Kippur, it seems at first to be the same old story of initial gains by Arabs met by crushing Israeli counter-attack. But this time the Arabs have a secret weapon: the oil-producers cut production by 5 per cent, and threaten to go on cutting until Israeli occupation of Arab lands ends. By December Western Europe is in crisis. Then OPEC quadruples the price of oil. For the whole world it is the end of a way of life.

The last day of Salvador Allende, President of Chile and the only marxist to achieve office by fair election rather than *coup*. Right-wingers attack his palace and he, steel helmeted, prepares to fight for his office. Later in the day he is killed – by suicide or murder? Picture of the Year, by an unknown photographer

Watergate: the scandal explodes – and becomes a
crisis. President Nixon, after dining with his wife
Pat, talks persuasively to the Press at a restaurant
(above); and his henchman Ehrlichman, looking like
a White House Mussolini, defies his questioners. The
"Louisville Lip", Muhammad Ali (right) was also
not saying very much: no longer The Greatest, his jaw
has been broken by Ken Norton. His manager weeps

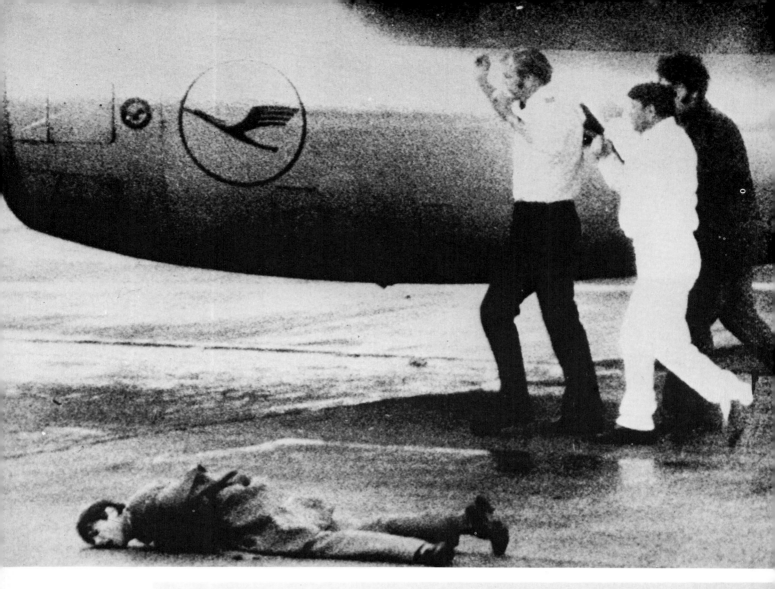

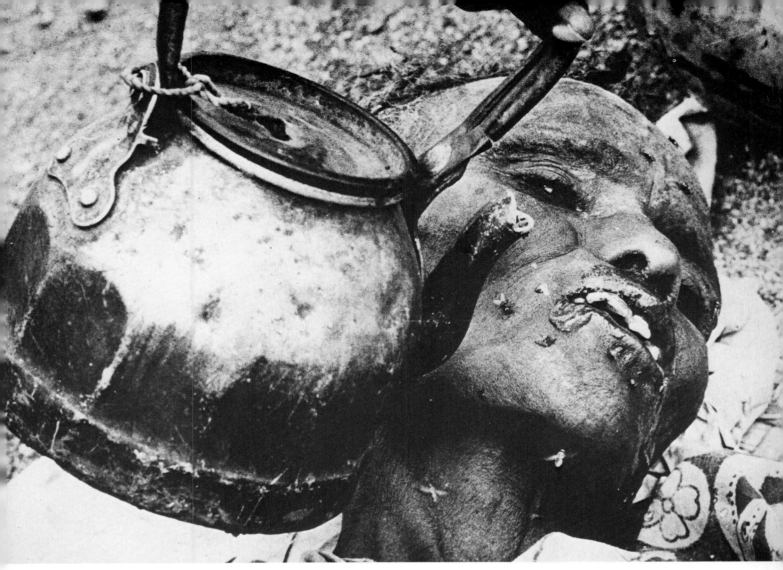

Top, opposite: one passenger has already been shot and lies on the tarmac in his blood as Arab hi-jackers at Rome force the captain of a Lufthansa jet into his aircraft. Such outrages do not help the Arabs fighting against Israel in the Yom Kippur war, in which many Syrian prisoners are taken (left). What does the trick is the Arabs' control of much of the world's oil: Italy's supplies, for example, come mainly from Libya. There (opposite, below) the ruler, Col. Gaddafi, prays in the desert sun with an aide. But new money flowing into North Africa from increased oil prices does not find its way to the famine-stricken Ethiopians, who continue to die wretchedly (above), oblivious to the fight for power in the country

Burst of sheer joy as a family run to meet their father, home after a long absence: he is Lt-Col Robert Stirm, and he has been a prisoner of the North Vietnamese for more than five years while his children have grown up

1974: THE NEW ORDER

Evening Standard
WEATHER: Cloudy. Lighting-up time: 8.47 p.m. to 5.13 a.m. Details—Back Page

CITY PRICES

London: Thursday April 25 1974

'Bloodshed if you resist'—seized radio warning

ARMY REVOLT IN PORTUGAL
Tanks surround Ministry

From Tim Brown in Madrid and Agency reports from Lisbon

DISSIDENT young Portuguese army officers struck at dawn today in the second attempt in six weeks to overthrow the government of Premier Marcello Caetano. Within a few hours the attempted coup was reported to be gaining strength.

The old order changeth. While Egyptians and Is- raelis negotiate, oil in the West becomes scarcer. In Britain a state of emergency is imposed as shortages are aggravated by a miners' and railwaymen's strike: Prime Minister Heath calls an election and is defeated narrowly. Harold Wilson returns to office. Inflation nevertheless gallops on. There is a blood- less revolution in Portugal, led by General Spinola, which ends not only the oldest dictatorship in Europe but also the world's oldest colonial empire. **Chancellor Willy Brandt of West Germany resigns** over a spy scandal, to be replaced by Helmut Schmidt; and in France President Pompidou dies, to **give way to the very different style of Valéry Giscard** d'Estaing. Haile Selassie, Emperor of Abyssinia, is overthrown, as is President Makarios of Cyprus, where a Turkish invasion leads to partition of the island between Greek and Turkish Cypriots. In Cambodia the forces of the communist Khmer Rouge encircle the capital Phnom Penh. In America the Watergate affair plays itself out with doctored – "expletive deleted" – tape-recordings which destroy President Nixon's remaining shreds of credibility. He is the first U.S. President to resign from office in disgrace. His successor is Gerald Ford, recently appointed Vice-President, who par- dons Nixon for any misdemeanour of office. An agreement with Egypt negotiated, Mrs Golda Meir leaves office; Itzhak Rabin becomes Israeli Prime Minister. The year is marked by disasters: 346 people die in a Turkish aircraft crash near Paris, and the town of Darwin, in Australia, is destroyed by a cyclone. There is a curious hoax, too: British MP John Stonehouse, missing and believed dead in Florida, is found alive in Australia. Like the whole developed world, he has money troubles. It is the only light relief the world gets this year.

Even in bloodless revolutions – and in Portugal the soldiers who take over control of the country carry flowers in their gun-barrels – the secret police of the old regime have something to fear. This PIDE man arrested in Lisbon after the *coup* knows how much

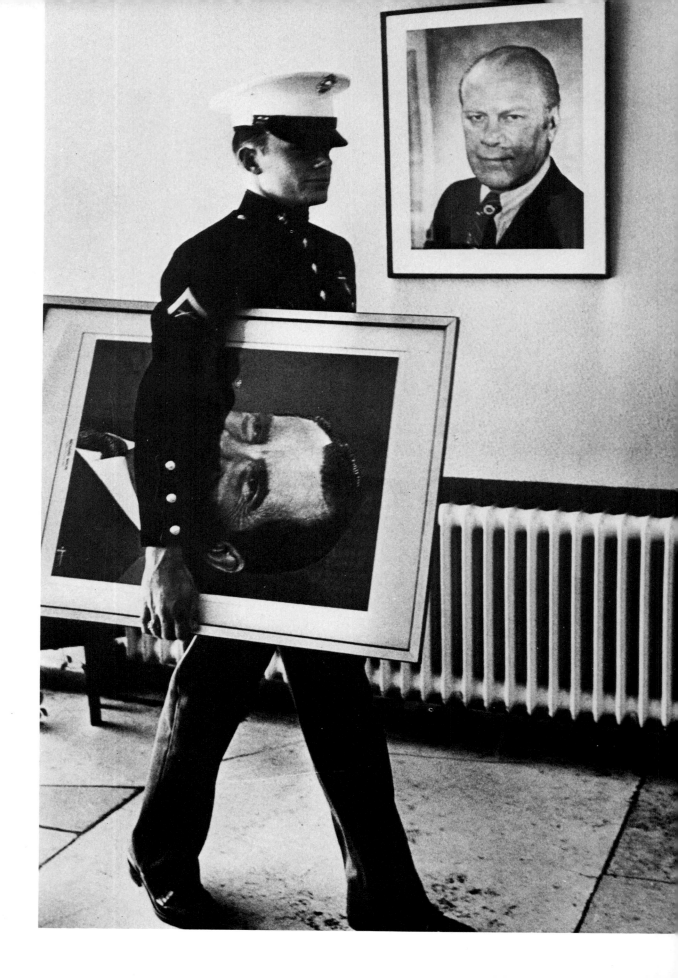

The U.S. embassy in Bonn: Nixon has just resigned after the revelations he has had to make about the Watergate break-in and cover-up. The official pictures are changed (left): but how did they get the portrait of new President Ford in time? Above: Ford in Japan, doing as the Japanese do – or trying to. The geisha keeps her eyes firmly in front of her and makes no comment. Perhaps eating with chopsticks is harder than the Japanese make it look? It is cruelly said of Ford that "he can't chew gum and walk at the same time", so slow are his thought processes; but Henry Kissinger, sometime Secretary of State, is out of a different mould: a meticulous physical clean-up does not distract his attention at the U.N. (below)

Yasser Arafat, head of the PLO, gives a triumphant victory sign in Algiers; but there is still no Palestine

General António de Spinola, father of the Portuguese _coup_ and, for five months this year, President of Portugal. Exile awaits him

In a corridor of the Kremlin, Senator Edward Kennedy walks with his son, who has cancer in one of his legs and must have it amputated. There is no great family so dogged by ill-fortune. Opposite page: Picture of the Year, by Ovie Carter. Drought and famine stalk in the Sahel, India and Ethiopia: in Niger, a mother comforts her hungry child

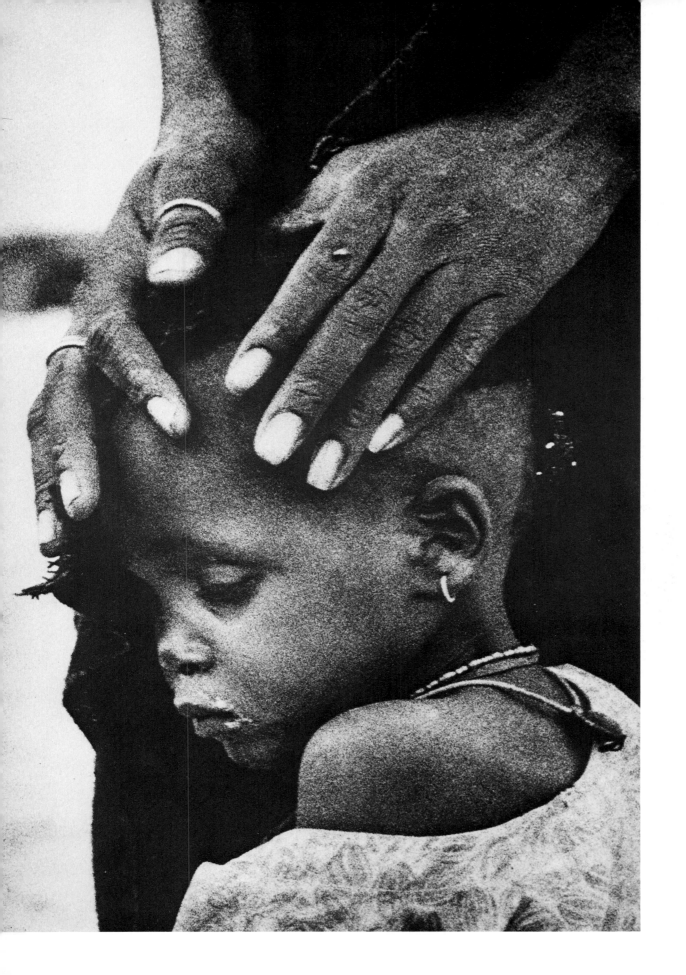

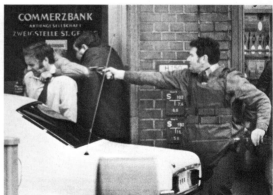

Left: Babies and war do not mix – but somehow, in Belfast, they have to co-exist. Above: a masked robber emerges from a bank in Hamburg with a knife at the throat of a hostage.
No-one dares to move – until a policeman leaps from a doorway and shoots him point blank

Gamesmanship: Johan Cruyff (above) protests to the referee during a world championship football game against Brazil. Left: the curious British pastime of 'streaking', as performed by Michael O'Brien at a rugby match between England and France at Twickenham

1975: THE NEW POOR

Now almost everybody, except the oil states, is a have-not. In the West oil-fired inflation rages. In the Third World, states that have nothing but raw materials to sell and oil to buy become poorer; but some find the big international banks eager to lend the flood of money from the Arabs, awash in the spring tide of their new wealth. The balance of the world economy changes fundamentally, and not in the West's favour. But scandals, *coups*, wars, assassinations and the crumbling of fixed symbols of stability go on much as before. Britain has second thoughts about Europe: but her people vote overwhelmingly in favour in a referendum. The Portuguese have second thoughts about their revolution, which becomes rougher and redder. General Spinola, its father, flees to Brazil. In India Mrs Gandhi is found guilty of electoral malpractices; she responds by arresting her opponents and declaring a state of emergency. Gough Whitlam in Australia refuses to resign after his government's defeat on a money bill, and is dismissed by the Governor-General, to be replaced by Malcolm Fraser. King Faisal of Saudi Arabia and Shaikh Mujibur Rahman of Bangladesh die by assassination. Francisco Franco, Spanish dictator, dies in bed, lengthily. Spain becomes a monarchy again under Juan Carlos I, a surprising democrat. Phnom Penh falls to the Khmer Rouge, who begin a genocidal reign of terror. The Vietnam war really does come to an end two weeks later, as Northern tanks enter Saigon. Of the American almost-empire in South East Asia, nothing remains but the scrap metal of war and the dead.

Nobody knows whether there will be another plane out of Nha Trang. The North Vietnamese are at the gates. A man desperately clings to the door of the overloaded evacuation plane. Desperately, a man on the overcrowded gangway keeps punching him away

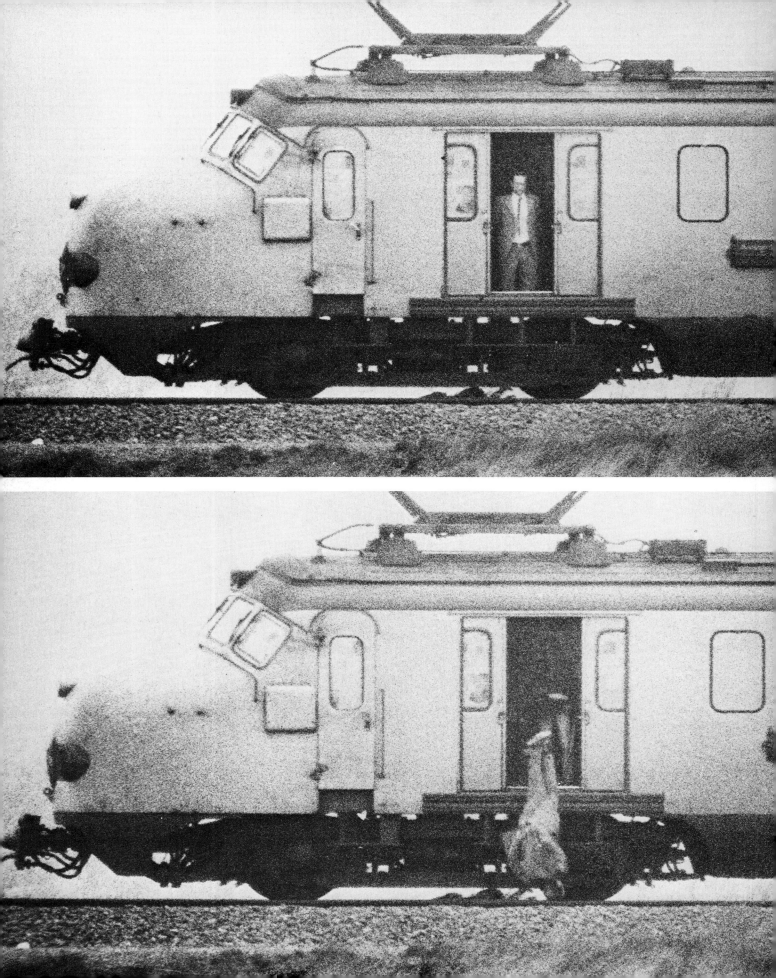

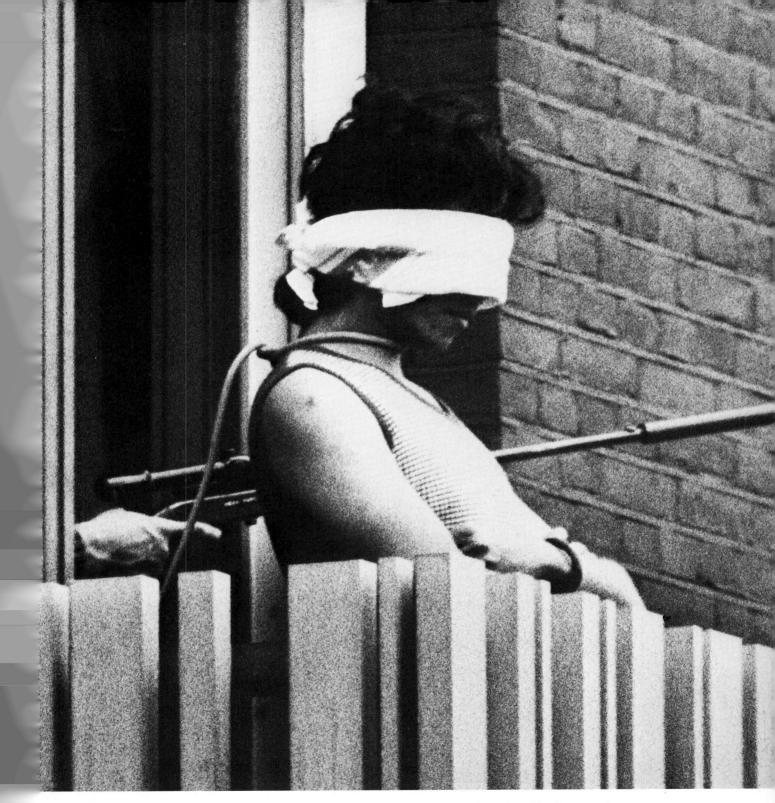

h Molucca, once Dutch, is now Indonesian; many South Moluccans living in Holland do not like this. e of them hi-jack a train and hold its passengers age while others occupy the Indonesian embassy. Their ands are that the Dutch should make the nesians give them independence. But the Dutch can do ing but wait patiently in the hope that nobody be killed. On a balcony of the embassy a noosed and folded hostage is stood, with the threat of h if nothing happens. On the train (left) one of the

passengers is made to kneel in the open doorway, facing the waiting policemen, soldiers and Press. Suddenly he pitches forward, shot from behind in the head, and falls dead from the train. There is still nothing to do but wait. Eventually other passengers in the train manage to persuade the terrorists that their demands cannot be met and all they can do is surrender. And after 16 days the hostages in the embassy, too, are released. Next year 14 South Moluccans will be tried and sentenced to long jail terms; but it will do no good. In two years' time others try again

An apartment-house fire in Boston: a fireman holds Diana Bryant, 19, and Tiara Jones, three years old, as they wait for the extending ladder to reach them. As it comes within reach and Fireman O'Neill grabs it, there is a screech of metal: the fire-escape bracing collapses and precipitates the two girls into the void. Diana Bryant is killed. Tiara, who falls on top of her, survives the fall. These pictures of the tragedy shock the Boston authorities into tightening up the city fire-escape regulations. Pictures of the Year by Stanley Forman

1976: GRIEF ENCOUNTERS

DAILY EXPRESS

No. 23,631 Thursday June 17 1976 Price 7p Weather: Mainly dry

President Ford vows vengeance after his Beirut envoys are dumped on seafront

AMBASSADOR SHOT DEAD

Express Foreign Service

PRESIDENT FORD last night vowed vengeance for the cold-blooded killing of America's Ambassador in Beirut, Mr. Francis Meloy.

And he ordered a review of plans for military units to evacuate all non-essential Americans personnel from war-torn Lebanon.

"As act of senseless outrageous brutality" — that was how he described the murder of also murdered Mr. Meloy, the economic adviser Mr. Robert Waring and their Lebanese driver.

Lesley's brother tells court of the £50,000 ransom bungle

Night it all went wrong

By Kingsley Squire and James Nicholson

A STRING of disastrous mistakes that Ronald Whittle tried to deliver a £50,000 ransom for his kidnapped sister, Lesley, was revealed in court yesterday.

The operation, said to have been worked to perfection which it was supposed to prevent...

The Chinese Prime Minister, Chou En-lai, dies. Change is in the air: there are riots in many cities and in Peking itself. In the north, a huge earthquake kills a million people. At last, after a period of sequestered senility, the Great Helmsman himself abandons ship. Mao Tse Tung, who controlled a quarter of the world's people, is succeeded by Hua Kuo-feng; who arrests Mrs Mao and three overzealous friends, the "Gang of Four", and begins to relax the ideological grip of Maoism on China. Britain's new Premier, James Callaghan, makes preparations to borrow £1000 million from the International Monetary Fund to avoid bankruptcy. In the circumstances, the first commercial flights of the supersonic Concorde seem a brave, if puny, gesture. But it is a brave act to travel on any aircraft this year: a French one, with many Jews aboard, is hi-jacked to Entebbe in Uganda, where President-for-life Amin greets the Palestinian hi-jackers. It is a mistake: Israeli commandos rescue the hostages and kill many Ugandans as well as the hi-jackers. Nobody attacks the athletes at the Montreal Olympic Games – but it is still a political occasion: many states do not take part because some of those which do take part have played games with South Africans. South Africa's own race-meeting is more deadly: in Soweto, outside Johannesburg, blacks protesting against *apartheid* education are met by police with guns, who kill 176 of them. The Lebanese, dividing into Christian and Muslim factions, are also killing one another. In Italy a chemical plant explodes, spreading a poison, dioxin, over the town of Seveso, which dies, its population all evacuated. In spite of all this, Jimmy Carter smiles and smiles as he is elected the 38th President of the United States of America.

In Beirut, the Lebanon, Maronite Christians and Muslims are killing each other, destroying their city and the country's government. Among the terrorised refugees a woman holds out supplicating hands to a gunman. Picture of the Year by Françoise Demulder

Two men who influence the young: above, rude Mick Jagger, idol of millions; right, sinister Charles Manson, idol of a murderous few

Crowd scenes:
Britain's Princess
Anne (above) at the
opening of the
Olympic games
at Montreal, where
she competed in
show-jumping. Right,
New York during
the U.S. bicentennial
year: people in
an apartment building
watch a sail-past
on the Hudson River.
Below, even in
Russia, among all the
swaddled babies,
one must be different

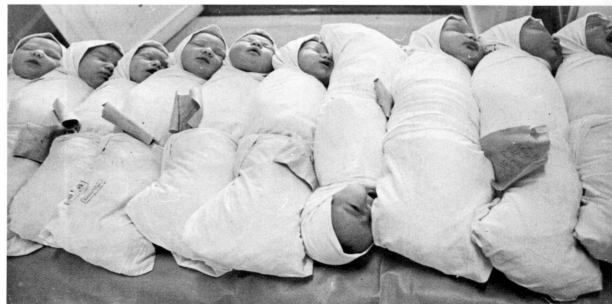

September 18, and a million people turn out in Peking to pay their last respects to Chairman Mao Tse Tung. Changan Street is cramme

with endless, uniformed lines of soldiers, students and workers for nearly four kilometres. The sound of their mass sobbing is unbelievable

In Thailand, demonstrations by students of Thammasat
University make and unmake governments, first of
the right, then of the left. And then they turn on one
another – beating, shooting, lynching, inflicting
mindless atrocities on one another in frenzies of hatred.
These pictures are taken as rightist mobs storm
the university: their bloodlust is not satisfied simply
by killing – the very corpses must be beaten, too

Olympic triumphs: Lennart Dahlgren, Sweden, weightlifter (opposite page); John Naber, America, 100-metre backstroke record-breaker; Bruce Jenner, America, decathlon winner

In Guatemala an earthquake kills 22,000 people and leaves tens of thousands without food or shelter. Help pours in from neighbouri

ountries and from Europe. Some of it arrives in small private planes – and one of them destroys the truck awaiting its cargo

1977: RULING CLASSES

At first it looks as though things are getting better. Queen Elizabeth II of Great Britain celebrates 25 years on the throne, to many signs of affection among her subjects. Mrs Gandhi's reign in India proves shorter: risking an election she is, to her surprise, defeated. Morarji Desai takes over and does not imprison anybody. Menachem Begin becomes Israel's Prime Minister and belies his hawkish reputation by being nice to President Sadat of Egypt, who is later to visit Israel and address its parliament. But the lion and the lamb do not everywhere lie down together. In South Africa the Black Consciousness leader Steve Biko is beaten to death under interrogation. In Pakistan General Zia ul-Haq ousts Zulfikar Ali Bhutto in a bloodless *coup* and charges him with murder. President Bokassa of the Central African Republic crowns himself Emperor – at a cost of £14 million – but likes clubbing prisoners to death. German terrorists kill a businessman; and later hi-jack a plane to Mogadishu in an effort to obtain the release of the surviving members of the Baader-Meinhoff gang from prison. The plane is stormed, the hostages rescued. Baader and three others commit suicide in jail. Hi-jacks become less popular. President Makarios of Cyprus dies, succeeded by Spyros Kyprianou: the island remains divided. At Tenerife the world's worst-ever air crash kills 582. For many millions who were young during the Fifties and Sixties, these deaths seem less significant than the death of a single middle-aged man in Memphis, Tennessee; but then he is Elvis Presley, the King of rock and roll in his generation, and he leaves no heir in the world of music.

Modderdam, near Cape Town: a black squatters' shanty settlement is being demolished and the residents, with nowhere else to go, demonstrate in protest. The answer comes from police, who rain tear gas on them. Picture of the Year by Leslie Hammond

Above: the sight nobody ever expected to see –
Prime Minister Begin of Israel and President
Sadat of Egypt exchange confidences in the King
David Hotel in Jerusalem during Sadat's visit
to a conciliatory Israel. Below: President of the
USSR Brezhnev has tears in his eyes at meeting
Louis Corvalan, *doyen* of Chilean communists,
after his release by the Chilean junta in exchange
for the freeing of Russian dissident Vladimir
Bukovsky. Right: a year to the elections – but
President Carter is already on the slippery slope

Leopoldo Aragon, a Panamanian (above),
sets himself on fire in protest at U.S.
control of the Panama Canal, and runs, in
flames, up the drive of the U.S.
embassy in Stockholm until he collapses
and his clothes are extinguished.
He dies within hours. Right: prisoners
from the Rhodesian war are held in
agonising balance by their captor's gun.
Opposite page: at Dubai the captain of
a hi-jacked Lufthansa jet is held
at gunpoint by one of the hi-jackers, who
later kills him, before the rest of
the hostages in the jet are rescued during
an attack by German special forces at
the next stop, Mogadishu in North Africa

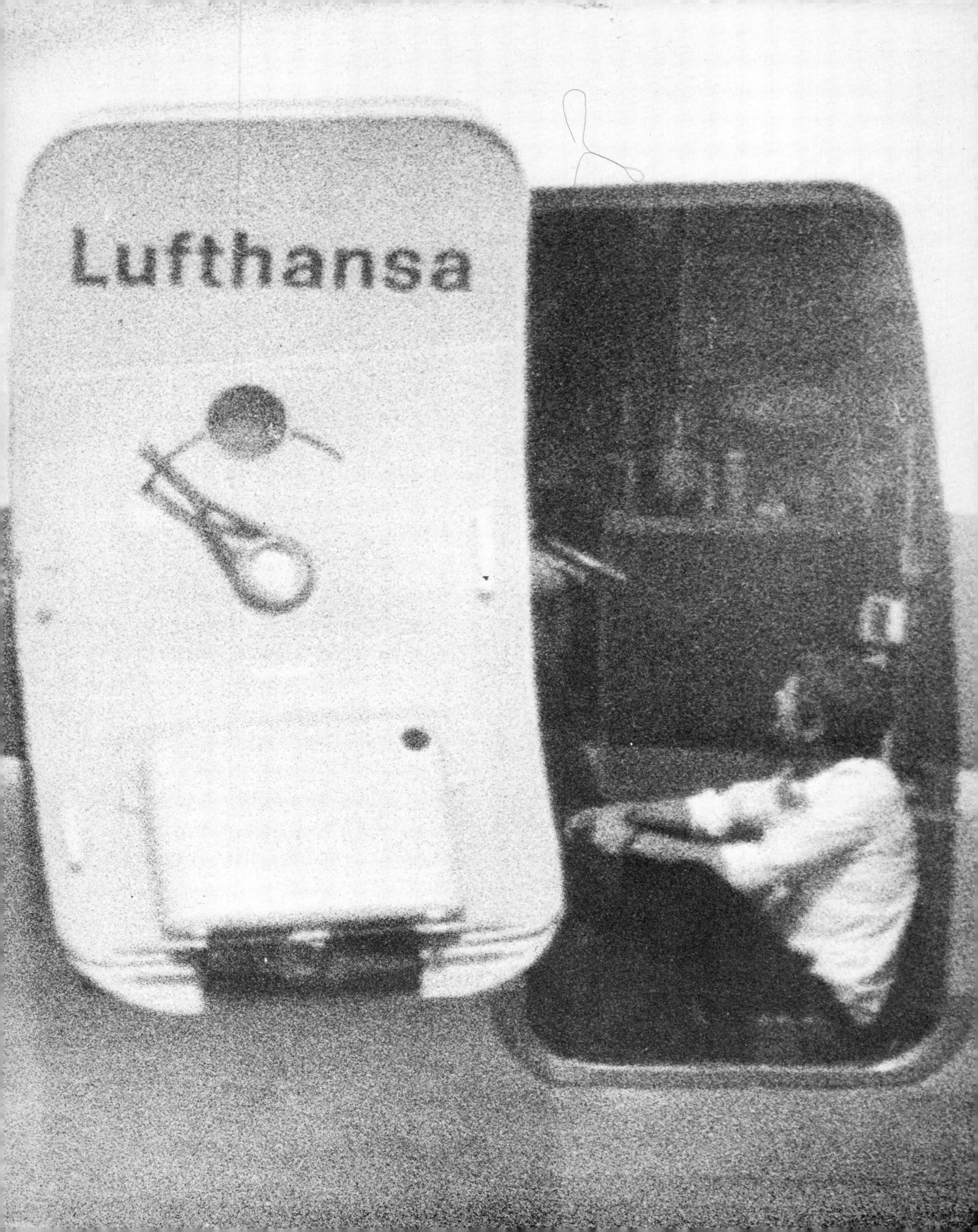
Lufthansa

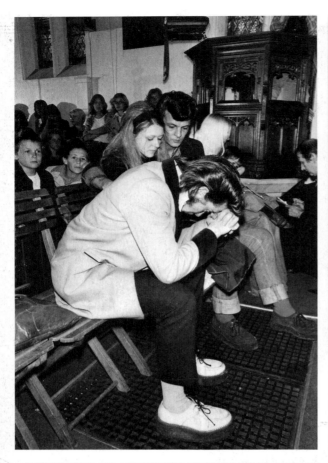

The King is dead, with no heir. The young, as well as many of those who were young in the triumphant days of his reign in the 1950s an

1960s, turn out in thousands to mourn Elvis Presley at memorial services. This one, in London, finds tears in the hard-bitten, even prayers

Left: the littlest gymnast in Moscow

faces her very first attempt at the floor exercises. Above: formula for self-portrait – press and run like hell

1978: UNNATURAL SHOCKS

LA STAMPA

Le Br hanno concluso con barbara ferocia il crimine iniziato in via Fani

MORO ASSASSINATO
Milioni di italiani scendono in piazza

La democrazia schiaccerà i suoi nemici

Agire con impegno sino allo spasimo

A world used to political casualties nevertheless finds something specially shocking in the kidnapping and murder of Aldo Moro, sometime Prime Minister of Italy, by Red Brigades terrorists. Even this is overshadowed later in the year as 900 followers of the Rev. Jim Jones are persuaded by their leader to commit mass suicide in Guyana. Less dramatically, Pope Paul VI dies, to be succeeded by John Paul I; who in turn dies almost at once. Next in line, taking the name of John Paul II, is Cardinal Wojtyla of Poland, the first non-Italian Pope for five centuries. There is grave trouble in Iran, where demonstrations against the Shah increase. Ancient authority is no more popular in China: Mao Tse Tung's *Little Red Book*, bible of Chinese communism, is attacked in Peking. Friendship with America the sometime arch-enemy grows, but there is gathering coldness towards Vietnam, which invades Kampuchea (ex-Cambodia) to uncover a mind-numbing story of mass atrocity by Pol Pot's Khmer Rouge regime. There are mollifying accommodations, too: at Camp David President Carter presides over peace agreements between Israel and Egypt: other Arab states are furious. In Rhodesia, Ian Smith embraces "majority rule" and reaches "internal settlement" with Bishop Muzorewa: the real black opposition continues to fight in the bush. Prime Minister Vorster retires in South Africa and becomes President; his place is taken by Pieter Botha. Little change is looked for. Extensive damage results in Europe from the wreck of the oil-tanker Amoco Cadiz off Brittany, where holiday business is affected. News of the birth of the first "test-tube baby" is received with mixed feelings by a world used to the consequences of "going against nature".

Whatever happens subsequently, it will remain one of the year's triumphs: not only President Carter but all the world – except the other Arab states – applauds the embrace of President Sadat of Egypt and Prime Minister Begin of Israel at the Camp David talks

Opposite page: "The enginer hoist with his own petard": student demonstrator against Tokyo's Narita Airport construction blazes as the Molotov cocktail he meant for a policeman backfires. Above, Aldo Moro, sometime Italian Prime Minister, lies dead in the back of a car in Rome after his murder by the Red Brigades who kidnapped him. Left, ten seconds from death: at San Diego, California, an airliner plunges into a residential suburb after being struck by a small plane. All aboard, and 14 on the ground, were killed

Portsall, Brittany: France's attack on the terrible pollution caused by the wreck of the tanker Amoco Cadiz is carried out with such speed and efficiency that the Breton beaches are once more usable by summer visitors

Blow the man down? But it is not just the
enthusiasm of the trombonists that causes Leonid
Brezhnev, USSR President, to hold on
to his hat on the last day of his visit to West
Germany (above). Luckily the visit itself
was less stormy. Right, black looks for each
other from rivals Haseley Crawford and
Donald Quarrie at the finish of the 100 metre
semi-final at the Commonwealth Games
in Edmonton. The cares of office have removed
the smiles with which Jimmy Carter greeted
his election to the U.S. presidency (far right)

Under General Zia, Pakistan reverts to "Islamic law" – which means amputation of hands for theft, stoning to death for adultery and, as seen by 15,000 people, public flogging for rape. This man and two others received twelve strokes each with a cane

White Rhodesians turn out to be tougher than the world expects in their defence of the privilege of generations: as guerilla war rages

about them they continue their peaceful pursuits – protected as well as carried for by blacks fighting on the government side

1979: DETHRONEMENTS

The "demonstrations" in Iran look more and more like revolution. The Shah leaves – "for a holiday". In his place, to wild enthusiasm from Iranians and foreboding in the West, the Ayatollah Khomeini, a religious leader, returns from exile. No inhibitions are felt about welcoming the overthrow of Idi Amin by Tanzanian troops in Uganda; of the Emperor Bokassa in Central Africa; of President Somoza of Nicaragua; or of the Khmer Rouge in Kampuchea, even if it is by the Vietnamese. But the Chinese conduct a brief punitive expedition in Vietnam. President Vorster goes quietly, unseated by scandal. The British Government falls and the U.K. entrusts itself to Mrs Margaret Thatcher, who quotes St Francis but looks very tough. The Rhodesian problem is cracked. By December UDI is ended and elections are planned. Ian Smith is unpunished. Had he been in Ireland or Pakistan things might have gone differently: Lord Mountbatten and members of his family are murdered by a boat bomb in Ireland, and President Zia hangs his predecessor, Mr Bhutto, in Pakistan. Pope John Paul II is greeted by gigantic and ecstatic crowds in Poland, Ireland and the U.S., each of which he visits with undiminished energy. Religious fervour in Tehran leads to the seizure of the American embassy there and the holding of its staff as hostages, for the Shah, or his wealth, or for fun. A reactor accident at Three Mile Island nuclear power station does not help America's bruised self-confidence. Almost everybody is glad to see the Seventies ended.

Sanandaj, Iran: the Ayatollah's regime has a short way with opponents. These are Kurdish rebels, who want independence for themselves; but prostitutes, drug-peddlers and even petty criminals are shot, too

Unable to stomach the new regime in South Vietnam, many thousands of the inhabitants leave, without very much hindrance from the authorities, cramming themselves into anything that will float. These desperate "boat people" die in hundreds as unseaworthy junks and sampans founder in the stormy South China Sea. Those that survive are unwelcome in almost all South East Asian countries, where problems already abound: some are kept on the beaches they land on at gunpoint, some kept waiting for months in quarantine in harbours like Hong Kong; and in some cases threats are made to shoot them out of hand if they attempt to come ashore. Some find refuge in Europe, America and Australia. It is a cruel footnote to the Vietnam tragedy

The United Nations has designated this the International Year of the Child – and in many countries special projects for child welfare are instituted; but in many others children go on much as usual, as beasts of burden and cheap manual labour

Northern Ireland: fixed at the instant of explosion by the camera, a bomb explodes in the Marine Hotel at the small seaside resort town o

Ballycastle, which has not been touched by the decade-long violence previously. Nobody is killed this time: and injury is slight

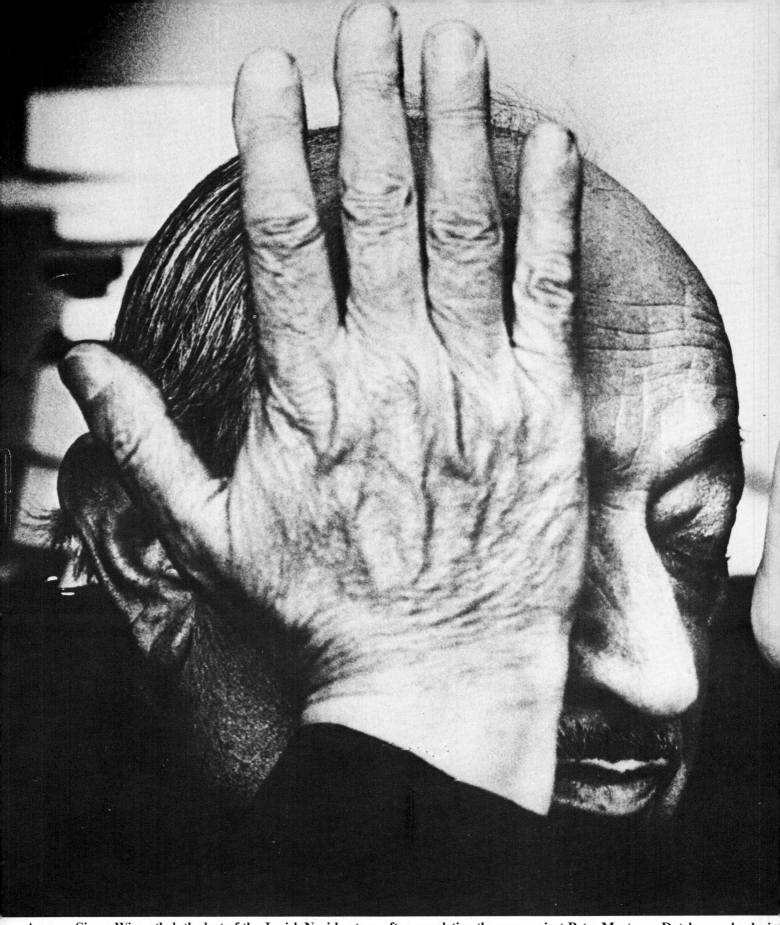

A weary Simon Wiesenthal, the last of the Jewish Nazi-hunters, after completing the case against Peter Menten, a Dutchman who denies

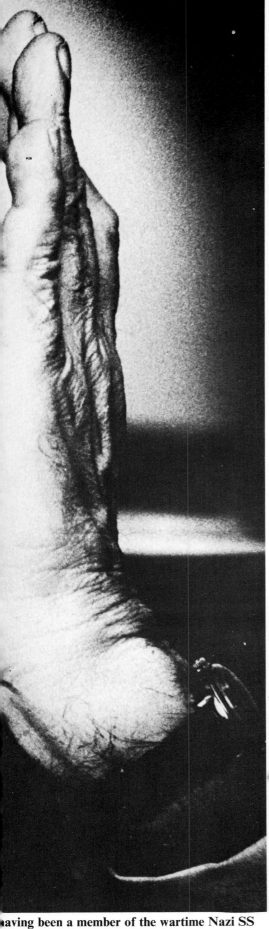

Above: Björn Borg, kneeling in gratitude for his fourth Wimbledon Men's Singles win.
Below: a three-year-old child, pulled from under her burning bed, gets the kiss of life

aving been a member of the wartime Nazi SS

A Kampuchean mother cradles her baby, waiting for food in Thailand. Picture of the Year by David Alan Burnett.

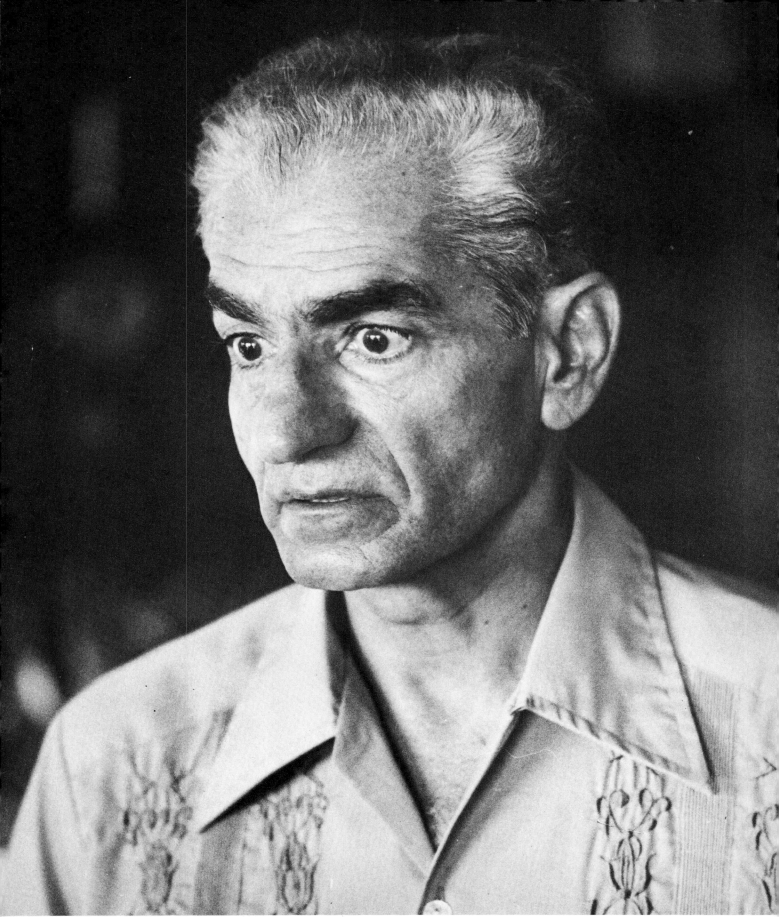

"The man without a future" – the deposed Shah of Iran in exile in Panama, already mortally ill and unwelcome almost everywhere

Cars friendly and unfriendly: a couch of joy for
Taputsa Mutasa (top), just elected in the short-lived
Muzorewa government in Zimbabwe-Rhodesia; or a
bludgeon in the hands of police (above) to drive a way
through anti-Shah demonstrators in America; or
a platform for a President as Jimmy Carter greets his
people in the small town of Bardstown, Kentucky

As Joe Rooks, television news cameraman at a drag-racing meeting at Indianapolis, U.S., keeps his lens pointing at the sliding wreck of a monster that burst into pieces as it hurtled up the track, the blower from its supercharger flies like a cannon-ball and strikes him dead on the spot

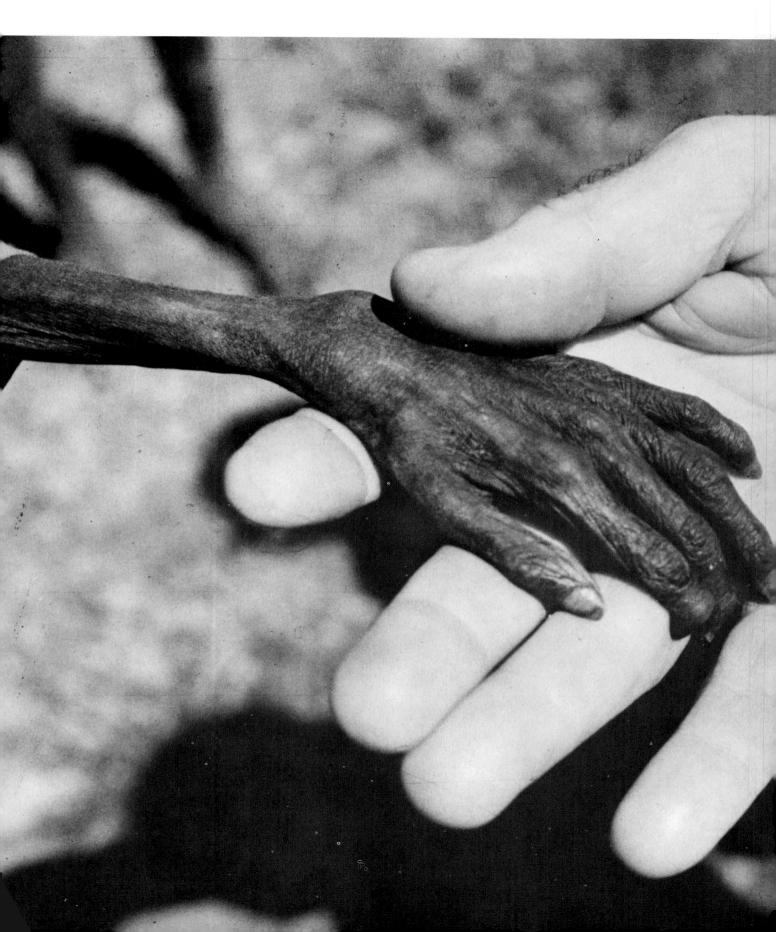

1980: BREACHES OF THE PEACE

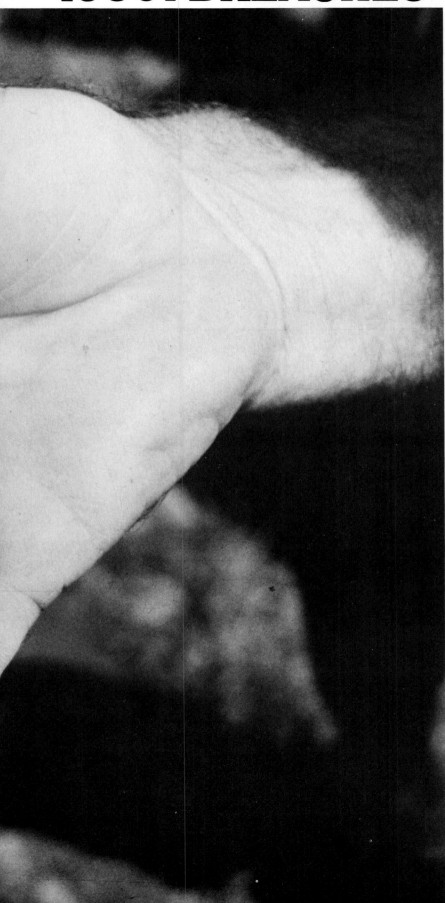

The Eighties begin badly. The Russians invade and occupy Afghanistan, to the world's helpless fury. Sanctions are ineffectually organised – chiefly in a boycott of the Olympic Games in Moscow which few but the Americans impose wholeheartedly. The U.S. mounts a rescue operation for its hostages in Iran; and fails disastrously. The Shah dies in Egypt: Iran then agrees to accept a $10 billion ransom for its 52 captives. Right-wing terrorists bomb the railway station in Bologna, killing 79. In San Salvador the murder of an archbishop in his cathedral leads to something approaching civil war. In London the Iranian embassy is occupied by nationalist guerillas, who kill two hostages and are then themselves killed – all but one – as British SAS commandos storm the building. In America a volcano, Mt St Helen's, erupts killing 63 and, allegedly, spoiling Europe's summer. There are earthquakes in Algeria and Italy, killing many thousands. Iraq and Iran go to war and rapidly come to a stalemate. President Tito of Yugoslavia dies, prolongedly. Sanjay Gandhi, in the wake of his mother Indira's landslide victory in Indian elections, is killed in an air crash. Milton Obote becomes President of Uganda (again). Ronald Reagan wins the American presidential election. To the surprise of most and the horror of some, Robert Mugabe, guerilla leader, wins in a landslide in Zimbabwe (né Rhodesia): he proves moderate and forgiving – even to Ian Smith. Spanish democracy survives. Kampuchea begins to recover. In Poland workers extract, by striking, huge reforms. But the year ends very badly for all who worshipped the Beatles pop-group: John Lennon, songwriter and singer, is shot dead in New York; by a fan.

The reign of famine seems endless. The Tanzanians have conquered Amin and ejected him; but the tribe of the Karamojong do not benefit as their traditional economy collapses. When relief does come, it is almost too late. The Picture of the Year, by Michael Wells

Losers and winners:
above, President Carter
and his wife embrace
after the election has
clearly gone to
Ronald Reagan – who in
turn embraces his
wife (on the right in
the picture). Far
right, Lech Walesa, the
leader of the new
independent Polish trade
union "Solidarity",
which wins unheard-of
concessions from
the government by the
use of mass strikes.
The strikers are on the
whole strongly
religious: below, some
of them are
confessed by priests
as they conduct
their protest rally

The West's worst fears
are realised when Iran and
Iraq go to war with
each other: the expected
crisis in oil supply
does not, however, arrive.
The installations
in southern Iran may burn –
to the great injury
of the Iranian economy –
but high prices have
resulted in a glut of oil
in the rest of the
world. Neither side in the
war, meanwhile, is
able to make
much military
impression on the other

Living victims are laboriously dug out of the rubble of earthquakes in Algeria and Italy; but it requires less effort to remove the dead victims of the violence in San Salvador, where mourners leaving the funeral of the archbishop – murdered in his own cathedral – are shot down by the military (above). In Afghanistan the guerillas who are resisting the Russian occupation of their country show small mercy to captured collaborators (left)

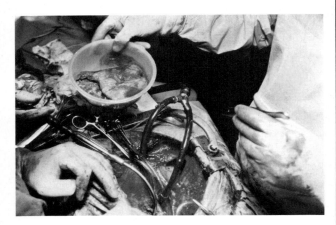

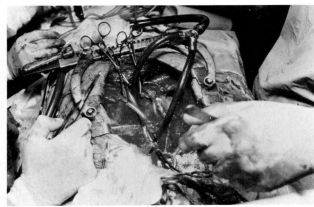

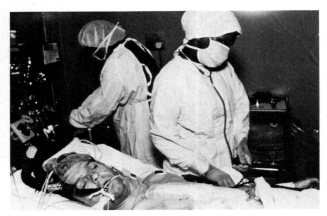

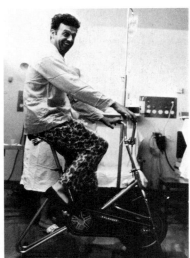

The transplanting
of a healthy heart
into a new body:
old heart out (top);
the empty chest
(above centre); new
heart in (right);
and the recipient
sewn up again
(above). Left, five
days after the
operation, patients
can take exercise

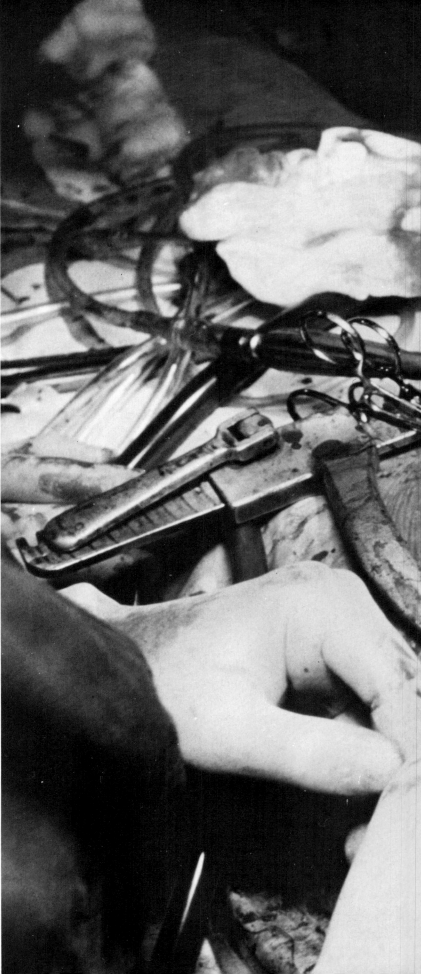

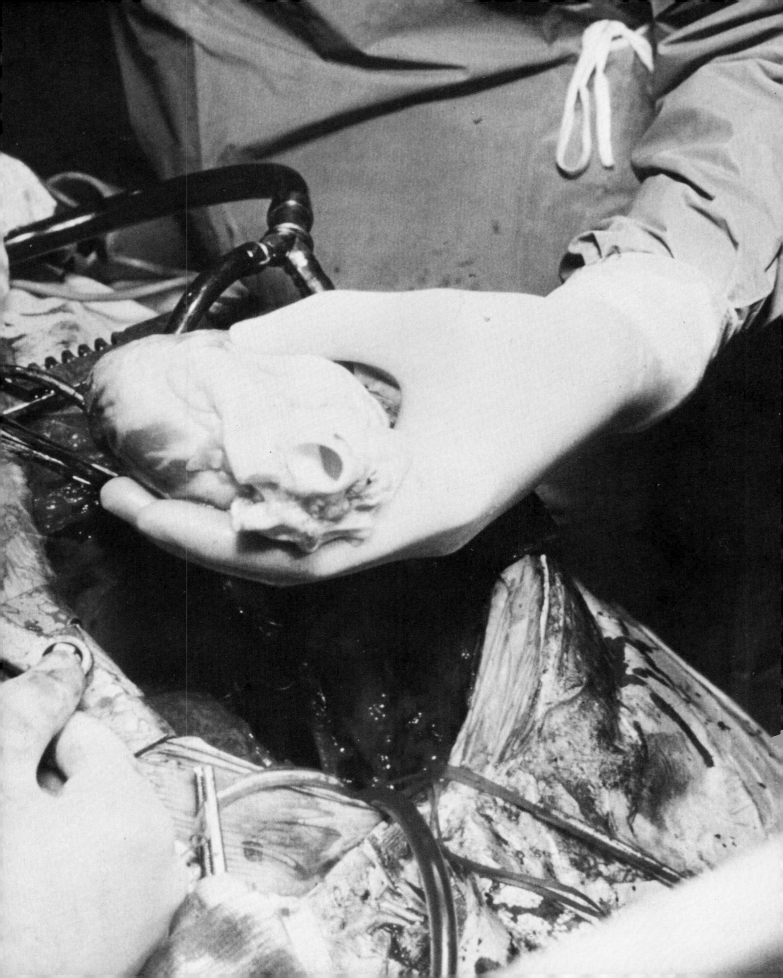

Athletic triumphs: U.S. relay team (top); Duncan Goodhew, gold medal swimmer, at the start of a race at the Olympic Games in Moscow (above); and right, the great win at the Games of Sebastian Coe of Britain in the 1500 metres

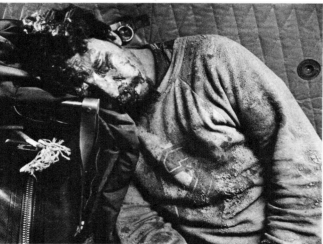

The most spectacular event of the year is also a massive disaster: a volcano, Mount St Helens in Washington State blows a huge chunk of itself into fine dust – which kills more than 60 people, destroys hundreds of square miles of countryside and much property and (so it is said) dislocates the world's climate to bring the worst summer anybody can remember to Europe

1981: YEAR OF THE ASSASSIN

DAILY **EXPRESS**
Thursday May 14 1981 • 12p • Weather : Showers
THE VOICE OF BRITAIN

The words the Pope whispered to a nurse after he fell
to three bullets fired into him by a crazed gunman

Moments after being shot . . . aides comfort the Pope as he falls back. One of his wounds can be seen in his left-hand index finger.

How could they do it?

THE POPE was fighting back early today after an operation to remove a gunman's bullets.

He had been shot by a young Moslem fanatic as he blessed crowds in St. Peter's Square, Rome.

The Turkish gunman, Mehmet Ali Agca, 23, was immediately seized by police, other suspects were also...

There was some occasion to celebrate during this year: the American Embassy hostages were released from Teheran to a hero's welcome back home, the Space Shuttle *Columbia* made its maiden flight putting America back in the lead 'up there', Spanish democracy survived a comic-opera coup and above all Prince Charles married Lady Diana Spencer to the delight of millions of television viewers the world over. Other images were more sobering in a year that came to be dominated by the assassin's gun: President Reagan in March and the Pope in May were lucky – they both made speedy recoveries – but President Sadat wasn't given a chance, dying in a hail of machine gun fire in November. Mrs. Thatcher faced hunger strikes in Ulster, riots in the inner cities and ever rising unemployment. Elsewhere – Mitterrand was elected in France, Papandreou was elected in Greece, but Poland ended the year under martial law with Lech Walesa in detention.

Above: President Reagan hit by a .22 bullet is hustled into his car by secret service agents. Main picture, Vatican security men assist the stricken Pontiff moments after the shooting in St. Peter's Square.

Top: Sadat lies dead as assassins fire into the grandstand with Kalashnikovs. Above, Mrs Thatcher in a pensive mood. Right, John McEnroe celebrates yet another Wimbledon Championship – how unlike 1985!

Opposite page, top: Charles and Diana ride through the streets on the first lap of their honeymoon. Below, President Reagan, as Commander-in-Chief, is shown a display of American firepower from his seat on the deck of an aircraft carrier.

she is 15.
the love every

PolyGram Pictures prese
brooke shield

she is 1
the love ever

1982: SURPRISE CONFLICTS

Wars in different areas of the globe continued to dominate most of the headlines – Iran and Iraq continued their stalemated slaughter, the Afghans continued to resist their Russian occupiers, fighting continued in El Salvador (despite elections) and elsewhere in Central America, and various struggles continued in much of Africa. However, some conflicts seemed to come from nowhere: in Britain 1982 will always be the 'Year of the Falklands' – a conflict which began with some illegal scrap metal merchants on South Georgia and escalated into a major war from which Britain emerged proud and victorious. Argentina, on the other hand, lost the war but returned to democracy as a result. Israel's imitation of Britain in Lebanon led to disaster – after early success including much destruction leading to the expulsion of the PLO – Israel stood accused by the world of standing by while Christian militiamen massacred Palestinian refugees in Beirut. The Israeli government has since learned the hard way that wars are easier to start than to finish. With so much war going on one might be excused forgetting that Prince William, a future King of England, was born, Italy freed the kidnapped U.S. General Dozier and won the World Cup, ex-KGB chief Andropov replaced Brezhnev at the top in Moscow, Helmut Kohl's Christian Democrats returned to power in West Germany, Felipe González's Socialists come to power in Spain, the Vatican experienced a series of banking scandals and John De Lorean was busted.

Far left: Villagers in Guatemala observe the victims of a death squad the morning after. Left, An ironic contrast in Beirut – an Israeli soldier takes shelter behind a wall of posters advertising more peaceful happenings . . .

Above: HMS *Antelope* explodes in San Carlos during the Falklands War. Right, The Queen and President Reagan ride off together at Windsor.

Opposite page: The drama of Ernst Baumann's fall at this important jumping event in West Germany was somewhat lost on the 'steward'.

1983: CRISES AS USUAL

Nasty shocks were once again a major feature in an unstable world. The United States and France both suffered heavy casualties when suicide bombers destroyed their headquarters in Beirut where both countries formed part of a 'Multi-National Peacekeeping Force' – in a country where there was no peace to keep. However, American troops had more success in invading Grenada. East-West tension – already bad – received another blow when the Russians shot down a South Korean Jumbo Jet – allegedly for 'spying'. Elsewhere – opposition leader Bettino Aquino was assassinated returning home, Mrs. Thatcher was triumphantly re-elected, Turkey suffered yet another earthquake, Nigeria expelled several hundred thousand Ghanaian migrant workers and Australia snatched the America's Cup.

Above: A Mullah shepherds a young convert past the sandbags in Beirut. Right, October 30 1983, a mother finds the bodies of her five children, after an earthquake in Koyunoren in Eastern Turkey. Picture of the Year: Bozdemir.

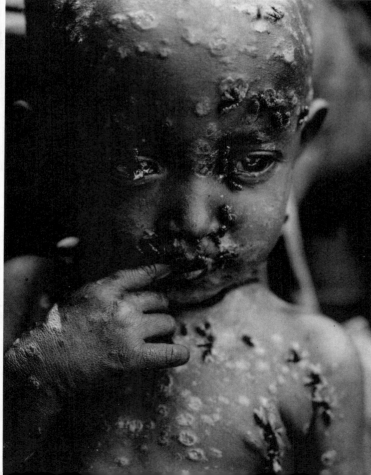

Opposite page, top: Assassination of Aquino; security men lift his body into a van after having killed his assassin (on the ground). Bottom left, Famine, disease and flies compound the misery of this Ethiopian child. Bottom right, Mrs Nancy Reagan seeks the protection of Mr. T from 'The A-Team'.

This page, above: Iran's leaders consider ways to victory amid the winds of war. Right, A child soldier pledges himself to martyrdom for Islam. Below, Mourners for passengers on Flight 007 pray over the spot off Sakhalin Island – eagerly filmed by the world's media.

1984: MIXED OMENS

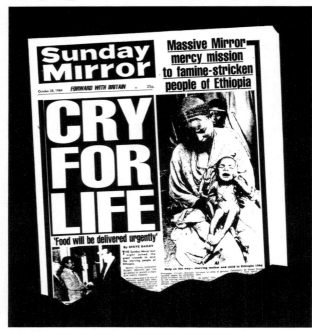

This ominous year, in general, failed to live up to Orwellian expectations. America hosted the Olympics in Los Angeles, which despite a Russian boycott were a roaring success and overwhelmingly re-elected Ronald Reagan despite the fact that Walter Mondale chose the first ever female running mate, Geraldine Ferraro, for the Democratic ticket. North of the border Pierre Trudeau finally lost power. Russia replaced one old man with another (Andropov for Chernenko) but remained intransigent abroad, Britain worked out an agreement on Hongkong, experienced its bitterest strike ever and nearly lost its Prime Minister and Cabinet in an IRA bomb attack. Latin America's huge debts continued to threaten a major crises in the world banking system. India suffered the terrible effects of the Bhopal explosion the worst industrial accident in history, and the assassination of Mrs Gandhi amid major Sikh unrest. Nicaragua was increasingly in America's bad books – looking increasingly to the East for help to deal with mined harbours and *contra* incursions. Ethiopia shocked the world with the depth of its famine and wars and misery continued in Lebanon where the ammunition never runs out, in the Gulf where Iran sent child soldiers off to martyrdom and Iraq attacked tankers with exocet missiles, in Afghanistan where tribesmen fought helicopter gun ships with old rifles, in Central America and in much of Africa.

Famine in Ethiopia
Age: 2 years
Weight: 3,000 grams.

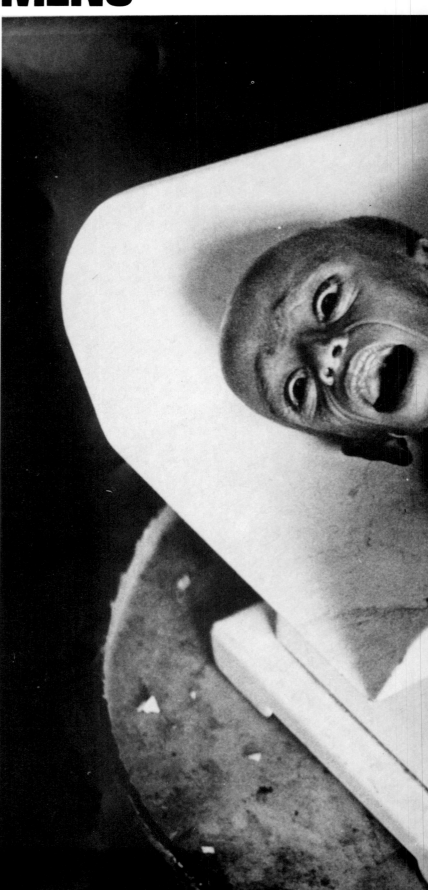

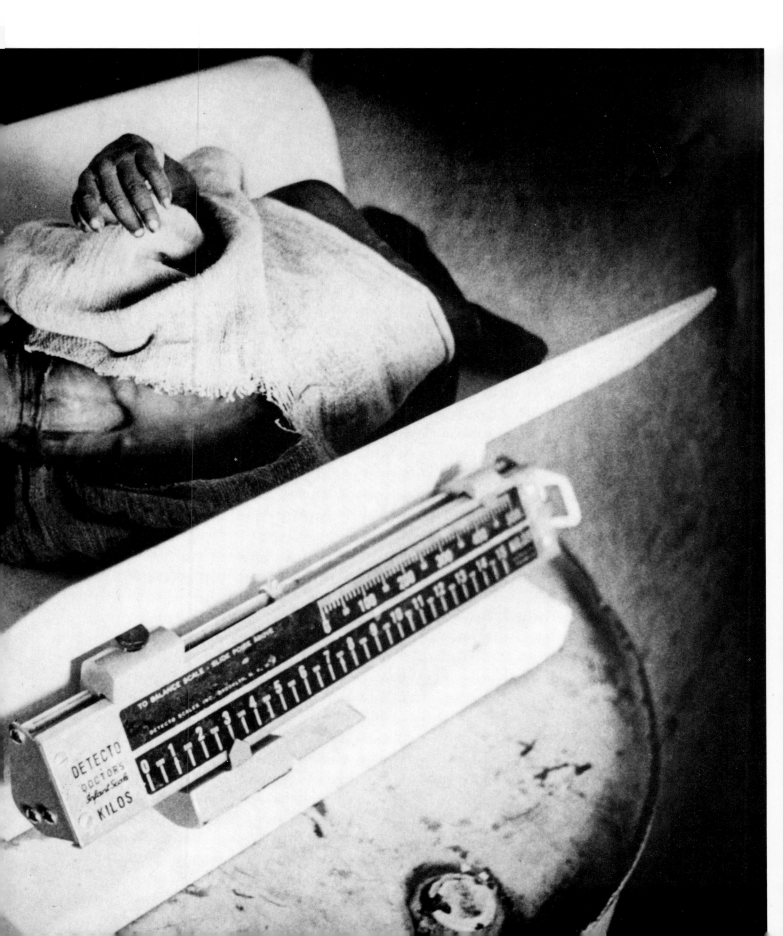

Above: Rajiv Gandhi at his mother's cremation. Right, a victim of the disaster in Bhopal. Picture of the Year: Pablo Bartholomew.

Opposite page, top: A refugee camp in Ethiopia – observed from above. Below, the miners strike in Britain seldom had a quiet moment.

CONTRIBUTING PHOTOGRAPHERS

Front page reproductions from the John Frost Historical Newspaper Service, Remember When and Mirror Newspapers

The World Press Photo Holland Foundation dedicates this book to the following jury members and to all others who have contributed to the 30 years of the Foundation:

Gerhard Aeckerle, Fed. Rep of Germany; Victor Akhlomov, U.S.S.R.; Y. Alexeyev, U.S.S.R.; Paul Almasy, France; Christopher Angeloglou, United Kingdom; C. Arnoldy, the Netherlands; Dmitryi Baltermants, U.S.S.R.; Istvan Bara, Hungary; Ettore Basevi, Italy; Anton Batanov, U.S.S.R.; Karl Beckmeier, Fed. Rep. of Germany; Juliane Berensmann, Fed. Rep of Germany; Walter Bernard, U.S.A.; Günther Beukert, Fed. Rep. of Germany; Mario de Biasi, Italy; Nicola Bibic, Yugoslavia; Harold Blumenfeld, U.S.A.; Floris de Bonneville, France; Karl Breyer, Fed. Rep. of Germany; Hal Buell, U.S.A.; Marina Bugaeva, U.S.S.R.; Daniel Casco, Mexico; Christian Caujolle, France; Howard Chipnick, U.S.A.; Simon Clyne, United Kingdom; Jan Cottaar, the Netherlands; Dick Coersen, the Netherlands; Sue Davis, United Kingdom; John Dominis, U.S.A.; Paul Dupont, France; John Durniak, U.S.A.; Alfred Eisénstaedt, U.S.A.; Sven Ekström, Sweden; Friso Endt, the Netherlands; Karel Enkelaar, the Netherlands; Harold Evans, United Kingdom; Paul Frederic, France; Heinz Frotscher, Dem. Rep of Germany; Bill Garrett, U.S.A.; Christina Gascoigne, United Kingdom; Yuri Golovjatenko, U.S.S.R.; Morris Gordon, U.S.A.; Paul Greene, Italy; Boris Grigoriev, U.S.S.R.; Fritz Gruber, Fed. Rep. of Germany; Alok B. Guha, India; José R. Guzzo, Brazil; K. Gyawu-Kyem, Ghana; Karel Hájek, Czechoslovakia; Norman Hall, United Kingdom; Helmer Lund Hansen, Denmark; Walter Heilig, Dem. Rep of Germany; Guus van der Heijden, the Netherlands; Hubert Henrotte, France; Aad van den Heuvel, the Netherlands; Lester Howard, Australia; Paul Huf, the Netherlands; Itsuhiko Ichiki, Japan; Colin Jacobson, United Kingdom; H.L.C. Jappé, the Netherlands; Orre de Jong, the Netherlands; Yu Junming, China; A. Katkov, U.S.S.R.; Mikael Katz, Sweden; Eva Keleti, Hungary; Henk Kersting, the Nertherlands; Dirk Ketting, the Netherlands; Willie Kleckhaus, Fed. Rep. of Germany; Derrick Knight, United Kingdom; Peter Korniss, Hungary; Yuri Korolyov, U.S.S.R.; Guenady Kovalenko, U.S.S.R.; B.

Kroutchtein, France; Charles Lane, United Kingdom; Th. Lepeltak, the Netherlands; J.-L. Lepigeon, France; Marie Luise Löffler, Fed. Rep. of Germany; Mochtar Lubis, Indonesia; Cesar Lucas, Spain; Bill Lyon, U.S.A.; Peter Magubane, South Africa; Vasiliy Malyshev, U.S.S.R.; Ove Martin, Denmark; Mr Masaharu, Japan; R.H. Mason, United Kingdom; W. Meier, Switzerland; Vincent Mentzel, the Netherlands; Akio Minamikawa, Japan; John Morris, U.S.A.; Heinz Morstadt, Fed. Rep. of Germany; Per Mortensen, Norway; R. Mottar, U.S.A.; Daniela Mrázková, Czechoslovakia; Hiroshi Nakanishi, Japan; R. Nieman, the Netherlands; F. Nosov, U.S.S.R.; Michel Nuridsany, France; Milton Orshesky, U.S.A.; José Pastor, Spain; Jacques de Poitier, France; Robert Pledge, U.S.A.; Mrs Plesko, U.S.S.R.; Eddy Posthuma de Boer, the Netherlands; Theo Ramaker, the Netherlands; Micahel Rand, United Kingdom; Albert Riethausen, Fed. Rep. of Germany; Lous Robert, the Netherlands; Bas Roodnat, the Netherlands; Arthur Rothstein, U.S.A.; Ladislaus Rózsa, Hungary; E. Schellens, Belgium; Kees Scherer, the Netherlands; Henri Schihin, Switzerland; Tony Schneiders, Fed. Rep. of Germany; Hugo Schöttle, Fed. Rep. of Germany; Kazimir Seko, Poland; Patricia Seppälä, Finland; Mr Simeon, France; Goksin Sipahioglu, France; W.R. Sjarowsky, U.S.S.R.; Jordi Socias, Spain; R.J. Spencer, United Kingdom; Bert Sprenkeling, the Netherlands; Dieter Steiner, Fed. Rep. of Germany; Otto Steinert, Fed. Rep. of Germany; Bob Steinmetz, the Netherlands; Olga Suslova, U.S.S.R.; Joop Swart, the Netherlands; Ad. van Tassel, Belgium; Joachim Umann, Dem. Rep. of Germany; W.G.M. van der Veer-Doyer, the Netherlands; Anton Veldkamp, the Netherlands; Gerard Vermeulen, the Netherlands; Helene Vester, the Netherlands; Piet van der Vliet, the Netherlands; Nils Wikner, Sweden; Robert Wittmann, Czechoslovakia; M. van de Wyer, Belgium; L.J.F. Wysenbeek, the Netherlands; Laure Wyss, Switzerland; H. Zachäus, Fed. Rep of Germany.

INDEX TO PHOTOGRAPHERS

The World Press Photo Holland Foundation most warmly thanks all photographers, their agents and companies who generously assisted with this publication. Every attempt has been made to trace and acknowledge all the photographs. If there are any oversights, they are regretted. The World Press Photo Holland Foundation, Weesperzijde 86, P.O. Box 51333, Amsterdam, the Netherlands, would appreciate any information which would help to rectify oversights or provide attributions for anonymous photographs.